Tom —

With Regards,

Ron

For anyone who has served on an ineffective board, *Zone of Insolvency* offers real and actionable insights into how a volunteer board can lead an organization and its executive to its proper future rather than helplessly watching the mission ebb away.

—William Janson, CEO, Keswick Pines
Continuous Care Retirement Community

Here's a wakeup call to all nonprofit board members and executives. Pursue mission without solvency and forget all of your good intentions. Thank you, Ron, for a concise, clear, and thought provoking call to understanding and action . . . highly recommended!

—Bob Kobielush, President, Christian Camp and
Conference Association

The cascading montage of penetrating questions asked nonprofit board members to consider, by respected and experienced consultant Ron Mattocks, are worth many times more than the cost of his well-documented Zone of Insolvency book.

—E. Eugene Williams, Ph.D.

Extensive experience in the office suites and boardrooms of health care and religious organizations has made Ron Mattocks one of today's most knowledgeable leaders in nonprofit management. His book is a GPS for NPO leaders, keeping us on the path of profitability and avoiding the route of ruin.

—John Ashmen, Executive Director, Association of
Gospel Rescue Missions

Zone of Insolvency

Zone of Insolvency

How Nonprofits Avoid Hidden Liabilities and Build Financial Strength

RON MATTOCKS

WILEY

John Wiley & Sons, Inc.

For general information on our other products and services, or technical support, please contact our Customer Care Department within the United States at 800-762-2974, outside the United States at 317-572-3993 or fax 317-572-4002.

Wiley also publishes its books in a variety of electronic formats. Some content that appears in print may not be available in electronic books.

For more information about Wiley products, visit our Web site at www.wiley.com.

Library of Congress Cataloging-in-Publication Data:

Mattocks, Ron.
    Zone of insolvency : how nonprofits avoid hidden liabilities & build financial strength / Ron Mattocks.
        p.   cm.
    Includes index.
    ISBN 978-0-470-24581-1 (cloth)
        1. Nonprofit organizations—Finance.   2. Nonprofit organizations—Management.   I. Title.
HG4027.65.M34 2008
    658.15—dc22
                                                                            2007045584

Printed in the United States of America

10 9 8 7 6 5 4 3 2 1

*This book is dedicated to my dear wife Deborah,
who never, ever, ever, gives up.*

Contents

Foreword

This is a "must read" for nonprofit leadership, both governance and management.

The reality is that the vast majority of small to medium-sized nonprofits are never far from troubled financial waters that can cascade into the Zone of Insolvency, because they live basically hand-to-mouth with inadequate unrestricted reserves and never really assured operating income streams.

The courts have put new obligations on nonprofit ships that enter into the Zone of Insolvency; hence it is in everyone's best interests to avoid the zone (and Ron Mattocks points out ways to do that) and to be very alert to roles and responsibilities when in the zone. Even large organizations are subject to unexpected financial setbacks, and shelf information of the kind Ron is providing should never be far away.

Ron speaks with the knowledge and authority that comes from many years of leadership and consulting in the nonprofit sector. I am delighted to commend this book to your attention, and I recommend it for your library.

Richard F. Schubert
Founding Board Member & Vice Chairman of
Leader to Leader Institute
Former President & CEO, American Red Cross
Founding President & CEO, Points of Light Foundation

Acknowledgments

This book flows from a lifetime of learning, shaped by leaders involved in all sectors of the nonprofit community. My heartfelt thanks is extended to all those who have contributed more than they realize to my understanding of the nonprofit community, and indirectly to this book, including Dr. Donald Bagin, the late Anne DeCicco, Dunbar Hoskins M.D., Bob Kobielush, the late Dr. Don MacCullough, David Noonan, Ed Nyce, Dr. Paul Olson, Rev. William Raws, Gerald Schiller, Louis P. Scibetta, Richard F. Schubert, Dr. E. Eugene Williams, and Douglas P. Zipes M.D.

I extend special thanks for direct help with this book to John Ashmen and Leslie Roberts for reviewing early drafts, to my daughter Holly Mattocks for research, to my son Todd Mattocks for the exhibit graphics, and to Gerald and Leanne Sindell at ThoughtLeaders International for coaching and inspiration.

What You Need to Know About the Zone of Insolvency

The Zone of Insolvency is a period of corporate financial distress, sandwiched between solvency and total insolvency.

The courts have expanded the legal responsibilities and liabilities of boards governing nonprofit organizations that find themselves in the Zone of Insolvency.

Board members and managers have individual and corporate liabilities for decisions made while operating in the Zone of Insolvency.

Since 1992, an increasing number of suits and settlements against boards and managers of for-profit and nonprofit organizations have stemmed from decisions made while operating in the Zone of Insolvency.

Approximately one-third of all nonprofit organizations operate in financial distress.

Until now, most nonprofit board members have never heard of the Zone of Insolvency, do not know whether their organization is in the Zone, and therefore do not understand their related legal responsibilities and liabilities.

About the Author

Ron Mattocks (M.S. in Management, University of Pennsylvania) helps nonprofit organizations build sustainable financial strength. He has a lifetime of experience in nonprofit leadership, management, governance, and resource development.

He has served as Chief Executive Officer of WICS, Chief Operating Officer of the Christian Management Association, Chief Marketing Communications Officer for the American College of Cardiology, Vice President of Member Services for the American Academy of Ophthalmology, Vice President of Marketing and Member Services for the New Jersey Hospital Association, Vice President and General Manager of the American Society for Training and Development, and Associate Vice President for Institutional Advancement at Rowan University of NJ.

Ron has served on numerous nonprofit boards including the Center for Multicultural Health Systems, Keswick Pines (Continuous Care Retirement Community), Christian Camp and Conference Association, the Middle Atlantic Health Congress, Haluwasa, and WICS.

He is founder and president of a consulting firm dedicated to building financial strength for nonprofits, and would be delighted to hear from you at Ron@MattocksAssociates.com.

Introduction

To pour forth benefits for the common good is divine.

—Benjamin Franklin

It has been my privilege to participate in the nonprofit arena throughout my life, as an executive, consultant, board member, donor, fundraiser, student, volunteer, and beneficiary. I cannot imagine life without nonprofit hospitals, recreational sports leagues, universities, art museums, charitable foundations, or professional societies. This nation's 1.5 million nonprofit organizations generate 6% of the national income and spend $1 trillion per year on programs and services. Their combined gross income annually exceeds $665 billion in charitable gifts, program fees, and product sales. They manage $3 trillion in assets. Together they employ 12 million people, more than the real estate, insurance, and finance industries combined (*Facts and Figures* from the Independent Sector).

Approximately 20 million of us volunteer as board members to govern these nonprofit organizations. On an average day, there are 20,000 nonprofit board meetings spread across this country convening in restaurants, hotels, schools, missions, and other venues where a few chairs can be gathered around a big table. Each nonprofit board is legally mandated by corporate charter to honor the mission and protect the assets of the corporation. Each board meeting is an opportunity to further the achievement of the organization's mission, enhance fiscal viability, and enhance the value of the combined nonprofit community.

It is perplexing that approximately one-third of these nonprofits, more than 450,000 organizations, operate perpetually in financial distress—the Zone of Insolvency—and approximately 7% are totally insolvent.

What are the legal liabilities and responsibilities of the more than 7 million board members governing these financially distressed organizations?

What is the impact of hundreds of millions of dollars given to charitable organizations that operate in perpetual financial distress?

Is it good public policy to continue to grant nonprofit charters that give license to operate forever without specific performance benchmarks or sunset clauses?

Is the nonprofit sector strengthened or weakened by differences in the law that protect nonprofit organizations from being forced involuntarily into bankruptcy by creditors, while empowering creditors to force for-profit corporations into bankruptcy?

Why does the culture of the American nonprofit universe have such high tolerance for financially distressed nonprofits, while European countries such as Austria require that nonprofits either generate annual net gains or lose their charters?

What is driving the growth rate of new nonprofit incorporations during the past 20 years at double the growth rate of new for-profit corporations?

Do well-intentioned businesspeople serving on nonprofit boards tolerate a level of financial distress in nonprofit organizations that they would never tolerate in their for-profit businesses?

Do board members have an inherent obligation to keep nonprofit organizations in operation regardless of their financial condition or their mission effectiveness?

Americans are a charitable people, and the community of nonprofit organizations has served as structure and catalyst for much of this charity. The annual output of the community of nonprofit organizations is a national treasure that has grown bigger and stronger since Benjamin Franklin experimented with the creation of one of the first nonprofit organizations, the University of Pennsylvania. But excess is the foe of access, and the explosive growth of nonprofit organizations during the past 20 years has resulted in an increasing number of nonprofits operating in financial distress. The net effect, if left unchecked, may actually be a weakening of the fiscal viability and service value of the nonprofit community at large, at the same time that the super-nonprofits have grown to multibillion-dollar enterprises.

This book is for leaders of all nonprofits. If your organization is fiscally strong, be diligent, continue to strengthen it, and avoid the Zone of Insolvency. If your organization has been operating in the Zone of Insolvency, you have three options: fix it, negotiate a merger, or file for dissolution. Living perpetually in the Zone of Insolvency, by default or by design, is a very risky proposition in today's age of board accountability.

Nobody joins a nonprofit organization to bury it. The notion of closing down an organization that has served many people over the years is fraught with emotions of guilt and questions of loyalty. But perpetually operating an organization in the Zone of Insolvency is riskier than ever, given the recent emphasis on responsibility and accountability for corporate boards, stemming from the WorldCom, Enron, and the United Way scandals, which led to the passage of legislation such as Sarbanes-Oxley and the California Nonprofit Integrity Act of 2004. There is no moral mandate to keep a nonprofit organization alive to honor its past. If an organization has served its purpose and is no longer viable, celebrate its history, close it down, and move on. If it is financially distressed but has long-term viability, fix it, manage the turnaround, and restore it to a position of fiscal stability and strength.

If you are involved with a financially distressed nonprofit, this book will help you identify common symptoms, solutions, and options. If your organization is currently operating from a position of financial strength, this book will stiffen your resolve to avoid the Zone of Insolvency in the future. It has been said that a disease without a name has no cure. Healing requires naming the disease, identifying common symptoms, and then working on solutions. Part One of this book examines case studies for perspective; Part Two names the disease; Part Three focuses on symptoms; and Part Four considers the cures.

Managing the finances of a nonprofit corporation requires more than positive thinking. As I like to remind my friends in the faith-based community, faith and prudence are not mutually exclusive. It is my sincere hope that in return for your time invested in reading this book, you will find practical tips to avoid entering or to escape from the Zone of Insolvency and you will increase your resolve to build fiscal strength.

If your organization is financially distressed, fix it, negotiate a merger, or file for dissolution, but do not continue perpetually in the Zone of Insolvency. We all benefit from the breadth and depth of the nonprofit sector, and it is in the best interest of the public at large that we enhance the financial viability of individual nonprofits and strengthen the whole sector for future service.

Ron Mattocks

PART ONE

Perspective

Where no oxen are, the crib is clean; but much increase is by the strength of the ox.

PROVERBS 14:4 (KING JAMES VERSION)

If you have ever had the daily privilege of shoveling out a stable, you understand the proverb. Oxen, the key to economic strength in agricultural societies, make a mess. And just like oxen, nonprofit organizations can be messy. In their absence, we could avoid the mess, but we would lose the benefits of their contributions to society. In this book are the tales of nonprofit organizations large and small, from healthcare to human services, from humanitarian charities to religious organizations. Whether generating $3 billion per year or $300,000 per year, their challenges lie in the areas of fiscal management, business viability, governance, integrity, visions achieved and visions failed. And these wonderful, compassionate, innovative organizations can be messy indeed.

Imagine 12 million staff and 20 million volunteer board members on the nonprofit trail, day after day, year after year, managing gross revenue averaging $2 billion per day, in up markets and down markets, in good times and bad. They advance and retreat, moving from offense to defense and back again as they negotiate twists and turns in the trail. The variables are infinite. Sometimes they win, sometimes they lose. Most take the high road, but some lose their way, taking ill-advised, ill-fated, or even illegal shortcuts. Sometimes the balance of powers and accountability designed into the board/management relationship yields great wisdom and protection. Sometimes it fails. Their paths wind through solvency, the Zone of Insolvency, and sometimes end in total insolvency or even bankruptcy.

Remember *Jurassic Park*? The story line revolves around the chaos theory of mathematics, which, simply interpreted, suggests that all systems have a natural tendency to spin out of control and settle into the dust of disarray. Dinosaurs will escape from secure island reserves, economic systems will fail, and the most natural state of organizations is chaos. Herculean efforts by board and management to achieve and maintain order may succeed in the short term, but every organization has an inclination to spin out of control.

Nonprofit leadership is a daily exercise in cleaning the stables and trying to keep the dinosaurs on the reserve; building and maintaining order in a context of infinite variables, delaying the free fall to organizational chaos. Negligence, poor performance, changes in market conditions, new competitors, or nefarious deeds can begin to unravel even the most successful organizations. We tend to be shocked by tales that reveal misfortune, mismanagement, insufficient governance, or legal problems. But the challenges are real, and no organization escapes from the harsh reality of the chaos theory. It is not a question of "if," but of "when." When your organization faces the unexpected challenges, whatever they may be, how will leadership respond? Will you take early, effective action to hit the challenges head on, or will the organization continue the free fall into chaos, falling into the Zone of Insolvency, or all the way to total insolvency and dissolution?

CHAPTER 1

United Way of America

BUSINESS OR CHARITY?

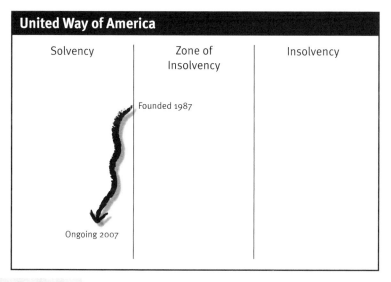

EXHIBIT 1.1   UNITED WAY OF AMERICA FINANCIAL PATH

In June 1995, lawyers pleaded for leniency in the sentencing of former United Way president William Aramony, arguing that his judgment was severely diminished by shrinkage in his brain and castration. Unimpressed, the judge sentenced him to seven years in prison for conspiracy,[1] money laundering, and embezzlement.[2] Aramony was found to have used over $600,000 of the charity's funds for high-priced flights on the Concorde, limousines left idling while he dined in fine restaurants, and consulting fees for his teenage girlfriends.[3] He was convicted on six counts of mail fraud, one count of wire fraud, and eight counts of interstate transportation of fraudulently obtained property (see Exhibit 1.1).

The United Way of America (UWA) is the separately incorporated national headquarters that coordinates activities of over 1,300 local United Way chapters, United eWay, United Way International, and the United Way Store. United Way of America's income is based on a formula whereby approximately .75% of the funds raised by local chapters are transferred to UWA to run the national office. Contributions to the United Way peaked at $3.17 billion in 1991, just before news broke of the Aramony scandal.[4]

A 1992 board-chartered investigation and report by Verner Liipfert IGI indicated that UWA operations had been "handled with an unacceptable degree of informality and deference to the desires of its two principal officers," and identified 10 specific areas of concern:[5]

1. Proliferation of spin-off organizations
2. Unjustified consulting fees paid to close associates of the executive
3. Travel expenses and reimbursement of personal expenses by the CEO and the CFO
4. Insufficient financial controls
5. The board's process for establishing executive compensation
6. Pension oversight failures
7. Inadequate documentation regarding donor-restricted grants
8. Inadequate controls over federal grants
9. Allegations of sexual advances by the CEO toward employees
10. Structure of the board

The Executive Committee of the board met on February 3, 1992, by conference call, to review this report and concluded with a unanimous vote of confidence in Aramony. Several weeks later, the same committee met again, rejected a resignation letter submitted by Aramony, reaffirmed the Executive Committee's unanimous vote of confidence, and requested that Aramony stay on as president and CEO during the board's search for and transition to a new executive. Attorneys subsequently argued that these two votes of confidence were implicit endorsements of Aramony's behavior.

Aramony tried to run the United Way as a business,[6] and in the process violated the trust of the employees, donors, board, and supported organizations that expected different behavior from the United Way as a nonprofit charity. By virtue of its national stature—raising over $3 billion per year through all of its entities combined—the United Way is blessed with a high-powered board that features many captains of industry and business. As CEO of the United Way, Aramony sought to interact comfortably with board members and donors of considerable wealth, moving in and out of their circles with ease and emulating their high-spending lifestyles.

It is reasonable to suggest that a charity should be run like a business, which involves implementing best practices to control expenses, increase revenue, and enhance the organization's fiscal viability. But nonprofit organizations are distinctly different from for-profit corporations, and management and governance must understand the nuances. The United Way, for example, is a mission-driven charity, totally dependent on donor gifts and sponsorship income, with virtually no fee-for-service revenue base.

In contrast, every for-profit corporation is based on some variation of fee-for-service or fee-for-product revenue, which allows for performance metrics based on volume. The nonprofit organization generates gift revenue based on goodwill and trust; the for-profit corporation proves or disproves its value proposition with every purchase. For nonprofits, individual donors feel violated when they see the lead caretaker spending money frivolously.

A media frenzy surrounded the Aramony scandal, making it close to impossible to discern the legitimate issues. His behavior raised questions that went beyond merely matters of "business style." Aramony clearly assumed that he was "entitled" to a plethora of high-end perks. In the mix were legal, moral, and ethical issues as well as conflicts of style. In the end, he was sent to jail not for conflicts of style but for embezzlement, fraud, and money laundering. The issues raised by the media were abhorrent for all businesses, but particularly toxic for nonprofit organizations. He tarnished the image of the United Way and reduced donor trust; as a result, charitable gift revenue decreased significantly.

As a convicted felon resting comfortably in federal prison at Seymour Johnson Air Force Base, Aramony had time to exercise his legal rights, arguing that the United Way of America owed him $7.2 million for salary, pension benefits, prejudgment interest, legal expenses, and costs. UWA countered by arguing that Aramony should pay over $30 million in restitution and damages. U.S. District Judge Shira A. Scheindlin ruled in the case of *William Aramony v. United Way of America* in the U.S. Court for the Southern District of New York.[7] Judge Scheindlin wisely pointed out that "A felon, no matter how despised, does not lose his right to enforce a contract. On the other hand, his recovery of any contractual benefit does not diminish the seriousness of his criminal conduct."[8]

Exhibit 1.2 shows that in 1997, just two years after Aramony was sentenced, the United Way of America (headquarters) generated a net gain of $1,266,511 on total revenue of $28,343,787, a 5% positive margin. But decreases in gift income in the local chapters were the ultimate outcome of the scandal. In fact, total combined contributions to the local chapters

United Way of America Revenues and Expenses: Fiscal Year		
REVENUE	**1997**	**2005**
Contributions	$2,813,037	$27,722,124
Government Grants	$0	$234,118
Program Services	$4,633,059	$2,699,811
Investments	$1,313,755	$614,735
Special Events	$0	$0
Sales	$615,465	$713,481
Other	$18,968,471	$29,742,859
Total Revenue	**$28,343,787**	**$61,727,128**
EXPENSES		
Program Services	$23,284,005	$40,523,096
Administration	$3,760,186	$3,878,878
Other	$33,085	$616,158
Total Expenses	$27,077,276	$45,018,132
Net Gain/Loss	**$1,266,511**	**$16,708,996**

EXHIBIT 1.2   **UNITED WAY OF AMERICA: REVENUES AND EXPENSES**

peaked at $3.17 billion in 1991, dropping to $3.04 billion in 1992 and $3.05 billion in 1993. Furthermore, the scandal was expensive. As part of its final court settlement, UWA argued that the Aramony scandal cost it between $11.7 million and $32.2 million in lost dues (i.e., the percentage of funds paid by dues formula from the local chapters to UWA). The argument, ultimately rejected by the judge, linked the decrease in local chapter funding to a decrease in dues paid by local chapters to UWA.

UWA argued in court that it was entitled to up to $40 million from Aramony, as shown in the next table.

$ 951,250	Salary Paid Out 1989–1991 During Criminal Activity
$32,000,000	Lost Dues Income
$ 1,804,085	Legal Fees
$ 373,653	Accounting Fees—Coopers & Lybrand
$ 140,426	Investigation Fees
$ 144,966	Interest on Loan for Payroll in 1992 Due to Income Reduction
$ 19,314	Teleconference Expenses
$ 1,126,767	Employee Resignation Program (i.e., buyouts for cost reductions)
$ 4,788	Videotapes
$ 30,089	Public Relations Agency—Hill & Knowlton
$ 25,748	Photocopy Expenses
$ 127,268	Cost for New CEO Search

Judge Scheindlin ruled that Aramony had to pay over $2 million to UWA, as follows:

$952,250	Repayment of Salary
$232,138	Payment for Damages Flowing from Criminal Conduct
$788,555	Pre-Judgment Interest
$ 50,000	Punitive Damages

In regard to Aramony's argument that he was entitled to pension payments from UWA, the judge ruled that UWA must pay him $3,221,057 for pension benefits and $1,177,121 pre-judgment interest.

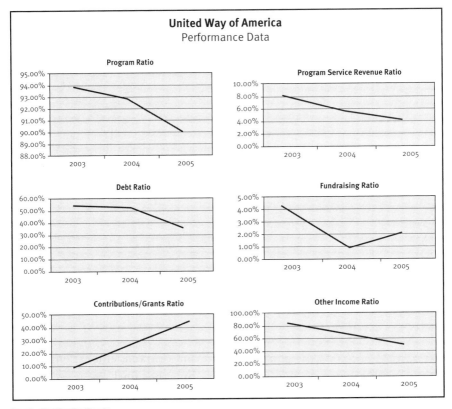

EXHIBIT 1.3   UNITED WAY OF AMERICA PERFORMANCE
                DATA

SOURCE: GuideStar, www.guidestar.org.

The performance ratios as indicated in Exhibit 1.3 tell an interest-ing story about the six-year impact of the scandal. First, note that the fundraising ratios are well below national averages, bouncing between 1% and 4%. The fluctuation over the three-year period could well be indica-tive of new management or a new campaign strategy. Second, note a sig-nificant decrease in program service revenue (i.e., fee-for-service revenue), as well as in the ratio for other income. As these two ratios decreased, the contributions/grant ratio increased to offset the reductions. Interestingly, the contributions/grants ratio increased significantly from 2003 to 2005. Finally, the relatively high debt ratio of 2003 had decreased significantly by 2005.

KEY LESSONS

Value of Board and Committee Minutes

Aramony, a convicted felon and a former employee of the United Way, was battling to recoup over $7 million from UWA. The biggest single item in contention was payment of pension funds, complicated by a change in the pension contract approved by the Executive Committee 10 years earlier. With over $3 million in play on this item alone, the Executive Committee minutes were a critical source of information for the court as it pieced together the intent of the committee in regard to the change in the pension plan.

Implications of Board Delegation

The Executive Committee minutes of 1984 made it clear that the committee had approved the pension plan change in concept and had delegated to CFO Stephen Paulachauk authority to handle the details of finalizing and signing the contract. The concept paper approved by the board included a forfeiture clause in the event of fraud, embezzlement, or felony on the part of the participant, but the final contract signed by Paulachauk did not include the forfeiture clause. Ten years later, Paulachauk was indicted and Aramony was in jail, but the U.S. District judge ruled that the agreement was governed by the signed contract rather than the board-approved concept paper, because the committee had delegated signing authority to the CFO. Because the board had legally empowered the CFO to finalize the paperwork and execute the deal on its behalf, the judge ruled that UWA must pay Aramony $3,221,000 in pension funds, even though the board believed in retrospect that the work of the CFO did not reflect its original intent.

Critical Need for Board Skepticism

"It was always clear to staff who supported him that he was a special, unique, and gifted person who had every right to set his own rules and standards."[9] The staff and board deferred to Aramony, and let him do so. Aramony could have benefited greatly from a dose of board skepticism along with a commitment to hold him accountable. Instead, board members who were outstanding in their own fields deferred to Aramony as the expert in all affairs of nonprofit charities and relied on him to bring the right issues to the board. As far back as 1990, several Executive Committee members received copies of an anonymous letter accusing Aramony of various improprieties. There is no evidence that they investigated the matter. Subsequently, immediately upon the 1992 release of the Verner-Liipfert IGI report, the Executive Committee offered a unanimous vote of confidence in Aramony, rather than delving into the issues identified in the report. Instead of taking a proactive stance investigating issues, the board appears to have repeatedly been in the position of reacting to the media and defending their man.

This tragic sequence of events resulted in an erosion of donor confidence in the United Way, accompanied by a reduction in total giving. Dealing with the aftermath of the scandal, UWA then spent millions of dollars on investigators, special audits, public relations agencies, and legal expenses while losing millions from reductions in charitable giving and chapter dues. But through it all, the UWA managed the financial distress and avoided the Zone of Insolvency. What followed was a complete overhaul of the United Way at all levels. As a result of the reduction in charitable gifts to local chapters and the reduction in dues paid by the local chapters to headquarters, the UWA was cash challenged, forced to borrow money to make payroll, and forced to offer termination incentives to reduce the size of the workforce.

FIVE GREAT QUESTIONS FOR YOUR NEXT BOARD MEETING

1. Are we as a board diligent in holding our CEO accountable?
2. Do we have appropriate policies delegating specific authorities to key executives?
3. Do we exercise a healthy dose of skepticism in carrying out our fiduciary responsibilities?
4. Do we accept full responsibility to independently understand and exercise our legal responsibilities as a board, or do we defer to executive staff?
5. If faced with a major crisis, could our organization avoid the Zone of Insolvency?

■ NOTES

1. Charles, Hall, "Ex-Charity Chief's Sentence Plea Cites Surgery, Shrinking Brain,"*Washington Post,* June 22, 1995, section B, p. 4.
2. "Ex-Leader Guilty of Taking $600,000 from United Way, Witnesses Depict a Womanizer Who Spent Lavishly,"*The Virginia Pilot*, April 4, 1995, front section.
3. David Cay, Johnston, "Court Rejects Former United Way President's Pension Claim,"*New York Times*, June 22, 2001, section A, p. 14.
4. Karen, Arenson, "United Way Holds Steady in Donations,"*New York Times*, August 19, 1995, section 1, p. 8.
5. *William Aramony v. United Way of America,* 96 Civ. 3962, August 4, 1998, pp. 8–9.
6. John S., Glaser, *An Insider's Account of the United Way Scandal: What Went Wrong and Why.* New York: Wiley, 1994.
7. *William Aramony v. United Way of America,* 96 Civ. 3962, August 4, 1998.
8. Ibid.
9. Glaser, *An Insider's Account of the United Way Scandal,* p. 192.

CHAPTER 2

Foundation for New Era Philanthropy

TOO GOOD TO BE TRUE

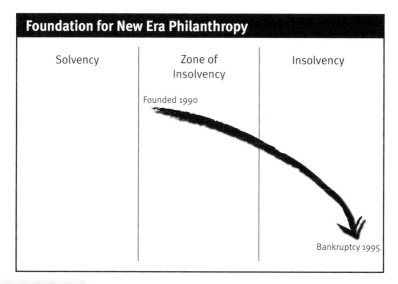

Foundation for New Era Philanthropy

Solvency   Zone of Insolvency   Insolvency

Founded 1990

Bankruptcy 1995

EXHIBIT 2.1   **FOUNDATION FOR NEW ERA PHILANTHROPY FINANCIAL PATH**

I n 1997 the lawyer for John G. Bennett, Jr., founder and president of a Ponzi scheme known as the Foundation for New Era Philanthropy, asked the judge to consider that Bennett was a religious zealot who heard phantom voices due to a personality disorder he allegedly suffered as a result of two automobile accidents.[1] The judge rejected that argument and sentenced Bennett to 12 years in prison for defrauding charities, churches, colleges, and philanthropists of over $135 million.[2] The federal government had filed an 82-count indictment against Bennett, who could have faced 907 years in prison if convicted on all counts.[3] Philanthropists defrauded in Bennett's scheme included Laurence Rockefeller, singer Pat Boone, former Treasury Secretary William E. Simon, president of Procter & Gamble Thomas Phillips, and Dr. John M. Templeton, Jr.[4] Bennett defrauded hundreds of nonprofit organizations by promising to double their money in six months through high-performing investments and matching grants from a secret group of wealthy philanthropists, which, it turned out, did not exist (see Exhibit 2.1).[5] Those snared in New Era's scheme included the Philadelphia Orchestra, the American Red Cross, the Salvation Army, the United Way of America, and numerous faith-based organizations. Prudential Securities, Inc. settled numerous lawsuits over its involvement in managing New Era's investments by agreeing to a payment of $18 million.[6]

Princeton University, Harvard University, and the University of Pennsylvania were all caught in Bennett's scheme. Penn was listed as a creditor for $1.55 million. Harvard had actually benefited by $467,000 and Princeton by $2.1 million. Both Harvard and Princeton agreed to return the funds as part of the final settlement with the bankruptcy trustee. It was an accounting professor at Spring Arbor College in Michigan, Professor Albert Meyer, who is generally credited with blowing the whistle on New Era. Concerned when he learned that the college was about to "invest" in New Era for the magic doubling of the funds, Professor Meyer created a spreadsheet from data he collected in New Era's (IRS form) 990 filing, and demonstrated that the foundation should have earned significant investment income if it really had raised the money it claimed to have raised. Professor Meyer then alerted authorities that he might have identified a classic Ponzi scheme and convinced college trustees not to participate.[7]

Line 21 of the IRS form 990 shown in Exhibit 2.2 indicates net assets at year ending 1995 of –$195,669,583. The bankruptcy trustee determined that the original 990 filing was fraudulent, and it took almost four years to reconstruct the financial records and amend the original filing to determine this figure of insolvency. Note that the lion's share of this deficit

	12	Total revenue (add lines 1d, 2, 3, 4, 5, 6c, 7, 8d, 9c, 10c, and 11)	12	145,044,273.
E X P E N S E S	13	Program services (from line 44, column (B))	13	156,971,337.
	14	Management and general (from line 44, column (C))	14	1,271,315.
	15	Fundraising (from line 44, column (D))	15	0.
	16	Payments to affiliates (attach schedule)	16	
	17	Total expenses (add lines 16 and 44, column (A))	17	158,242,652.
A S S E T S	18	Excess or (deficit) for the year (subtract line 17 from line 12)	18	-13,198,379.
N E T	19	Net assets or fund balances at beginning of year (from line 73, column (A))	19	-182,471,204.
	20	Other changes in net assets or fund balances (attach explanation)	20	
	21	Net assets or fund balances at end of year (combine lines 18, 19, and 20)	21	-195,669,583.

BAA For Paperwork Reduction Act Notice, see instructions.   Form 990 (1995)

EXHIBIT 2.2   **FOUNDATION FOR NEW ERA PHILANTHROPY FORM 990 NET ASSETS**

carried over from previous years, with an additional $13,000,000 deficit piled on in 1995. This was an organization with a history of financial woes, not a sudden onset of financial distress.

For those of you who think that reading tax filings is boring, this one may change your mind. Remember that the bankruptcy trustee determined that the original 990 filing for 1995 was fraudulent, so he reconstructed the financial records and amended the filing in 1999. In Part II, Compensation of the Five Highest Paid Independent Contractors for Professional Services, the trustee determined that Bennett had helped himself to a consulting fee of $1,175,000. As if that fee alone were not embarrassing enough, by the time the amended 990 was filed, the legal address for Bennett, listed in Exhibit 2.3, was the Federal Institute of Correction, Fort Dix, NJ.

One of the great surprises in a case like this is how quickly the fraudulent enterprise can ramp up its activity level. In Exhibit 2.4, we see that contributions (investments) to New Era spiraled from $2,600,000 in 1991 to $9,400,000 in 1992, $41,600,000 in 1993, and $160,100,000 in 1994. Obviously, the word-of-mouth power of the miraculous doubling of the funds had started to drive more and more investors to New Era. Mr. Bennett's offer to double each nonprofit organization's investment in six months was simply too good to be true. Given the prestigious list of organizations that were duped into investing in order to double their money, it must have been a great sales pitch. The nonprofit community is very close knit, and the word-of-mouth publicity about New Era's anonymous big donors who were matching gifts to help New Era double

Part II Compensation of the Five Highest Paid Independent Contractors for Professional Services (See instructions. List each one (whether individuals or firms). If there are none, enter 'None.')		
(a) Name and address of each independent contractor paid more than $50,000	(b) Type of service	(c) Compensation
J. DOUGLAS HOLLADAY		
4786 OLD DOMINION DR. ARLINGTON, VA 22207	CONSULT./TECH ADV.	72,917.
LAUREL COMMUNICATIONS		
201 LAURENCE DR. MOORESTOWN, NJ 08057	CONSULT./TECH ADV.	65,832.
RWO ASSOCIATES		
414 MILL CREEK RD. GLADWYNE, PA 19035	CONSULT./TECH ADV.	83,335.
BENNETT GRP. INTNL., LTD C/O JOHN G. BENNETT		
FEDERAL INSTITUTE OF CORRECTION, FORT DIX, NJ	CONSULT./TECH ADV.	1,175,000.
Total number of others receiving over $50,000 for professional services .... ►NONE		

BAA For Paperwork Reduction Act Notice, see the instructions to Form 990 (or Form 990-EZ).   Schedule A (Form 990) 1995

EXHIBIT 2.3   COMPENSATION OF THE FIVE HIGHEST-PAID INDEPENDENT CONTRACTORS FOR PROFESSIONAL SERVICES

the money for one organization after another soon made believers out of a very conservative community, as more and more organizations stepped up to invest dollars in New Era for the magical doubling of funds in six months. In the end, paying off investors with the funds of new investors, Bennett's classic Ponzi scheme had racked up over $500 million in liabilities against less than $100 million in assets.

At his sentencing hearing, Mr. Bennett told the U.S. District judge, "I'm a disaster financially. . . . I'm just very bad at handling details,

Schedule A (Form 990) 1995 FOUNDATION FOR NEW ERA PHILANTHROPY 23-2578189 Page 3				
Part IV-A Support Schedule (Complete only if you checked a box on line 10, 11, or 12.) Use cash method of accounting. Note :You may use the worksheet in the instructions for converting from the accrual to the cash method of accounting.				
Calendar year (or fiscal year beginning in) ►	(a) 1994	(b) 1993	(c) 1992	(d) 1991	(e) Total
15 Gifts, grants, and contributions received. (Do not include unusual grants. See line 28.) ...	160,141,656.	41,665,556.	9,369,017.	2,616,847.	213,793,076.

EXHIBIT 2.4   CONTRIBUTIONS TO NEW ERA FROM 1991 TO 1994

handling money, the record keeping of it. . . . I'm more interested in the ideas." He went on to describe himself as unable to say no to requests for help, having a history of making promises he could not keep, and seeing nothing wrong with writing checks when he did not have the funds to cover them.[8] Based on Exhibit 2.3, his financial shortcomings were not so great that he couldn't peel out $1,750,000 for his own personal use in 1995. The Securities and Exchange Commission estimated that $4.2 million of charity money found its way to Bennett's personal accounts.[9]

Philadelphia mayor Ed Rendell said Bennett "seemed to be a wonderful guy." The mayor, who knew Bennett and spoke to him directly about his fundraising activities in Philadelphia, said, "I was counting on Jack to push us over the top, to make Philadelphia the best destination city in the Northeast."[10]

Robert Montgomery Scott, president of the Philadelphia Art Museum, was often odd man out in discussions about New Era because of his skepticism. "Show me the prospectus," Mr. Scott would say.[11] Apparently the prospectus never surfaced, and Mr. Scott managed to avoid involving the Philadelphia Art Museum in New Era's snare.

Dr. Gilbert Peterson, the highly regarded president of Lancaster Bible College, known for his fiscally conservative, no-nonsense management style, found that the college was out over $16 million when the music stopped at New Era. Introduced to New Era by a friend, Dr. Peterson was originally skeptical. "We checked out every source, looked over their records, and talked to other institutions who were participating in the program," Peterson said. "It looked like an outstanding opportunity."[12]

"We participated only after careful deliberations by the executive committee of the board of trustees," said a spokesman for Gordon College. "The board reviewed documents, checked references, and even contacted the Pennsylvania State Attorney General's office."[13]

"We did some homework and found these great results and references," said Paul Nelson, president of the Evangelical Council for Financial Accountability (ECFA). "All said, he's a wonderful person who wants to do good." Approximately 100 of the organizations victimized by New Era were members of ECFA.[14]

"There's tremendous pressure on charities today to increase their revenues to meet expenses and growing public needs," said Bennett M. Weiner, head of Philanthropic Advisory Service and Council of Better Business Bureaus.

"Unfortunately, this can influence some organizations to take financial risks because of the potential rewards."[15]

"It proves that experienced people are as foolish as anyone else. It was a foundation in name only. It had no assets. A lot of it is done on the cumulative weight of people who had a good experience. People make their decision based on talking to other people," said Charles L. Andes, chief executive of a database marketing company and a New Era creditor.[16]

"It's not crazy. People are very busy. People you respect are in it. They vouch for it," said a former partner at Goldman, Sachs.[17]

There were three critical signs that should have served as warnings to over 600 organizations and individuals who were defrauded by New Era. First, the financial reporting for the six years New Era operated included just one annual report, minimal financial statements, only one financial audit, failure to file tax returns, and failure to identify board members. As evident in Exhibit 2.5, the losses began to accrue as early as 1991 and should have raised questions of solvency. Second, New Era did not register with the state charities office until four years after it incorporated, and never registered as a professional solicitor to raise funds. Third, the fact that "investors" were required to put money into a New Era brokerage account for six months in order to double their money and the fact that these funds were commingled and not in separate escrow accounts should have set off warning sirens.

So where was the board that should have had policies governing New Era's activities and should have been holding Bennett accountable?

And where were the boards of the hundreds of nonprofit organizations that either benefited from or lost money through investing with New Era? Certainly most if not all of these boards had investment policies to which they would hold their managers accountable. Why did so many organizations take such a disproportionately high risk? Why were there not policies enforced by the boards in regard to investment and risk? Why would management overlook these policies and take such a risk? Was the sales pitch that good? Were the verbal endorsements from peer organizations that had profited so convincing? Was the allure of doubling the money that strong?

New Era's top nonprofit creditors, according to the bankruptcy trustee, included the following:

EXHIBIT 2.5   **BALANCE SHEET FOR FISCAL YEAR ENDING DECEMBER 31, 1991**

Foundation for New Era Philanthropy
Balance Sheet for fiscal Year Ending December 31, 1991

ASSETS	January 1, 1991	December 31, 1991	Change
Cash & Equivalent	$4,312	$166,856	$162,544
Accounts Receivable	$0	$0	$0
Pledges & Grants Receivable	$400,000	$302,055	($97,945)
Receivable/Other	$14,793	$0	($14,793)
Inventories for Sale of Use	$0	$0	$0
Investment/Securities	$12,466	$29,110	$16,644
Investment/Other	$0	$0	$0
Fixed Assets	$2,014	$12,743	$10,729
Other	$0	$0	$0
Total Assets	**$433,585**	**$510,764**	**$77,179**
LIABILITIES			
Accounts Payable	$0	$0	$0
Grants Payable	$392,950	$2,610,000	$2,217,050
Deferred Revenue	$0	$0	$0
Loans and Notes	$0	$0	$0
Tax-Exempt Bond Liabilities	$0	$0	$0
Other	$0	$0	$0
Total Liabilities	$392,950	$2,610,000	2,217,050
Fund Balance	**$40,635**	**($2,099,236)**	**($2,139,871)**

- Lancaster Bible College—$16,900,000
- Young Life International—$11,000,000
- The Maclellan Foundation—$8,500,000
- Cornerstone Trust—$8,000,000
- Philadelphia Orchestra Association—$8,000,000
- Philadelphia College of Bible—$8,000,000
- Whitworth College—$7,000,000
- Academy of Natural Sciences—$6,700,000
- Drexel University—$6,000,000

This tragic tale wound its way through the Zone of Insolvency and ended in bankruptcy and dissolution for New Era, a prison sentence for Mr. Bennett, and loss of funds for hundreds of organizations and individual philanthropists who had been duped. The good work of the bankruptcy trustee, combined with the goodwill of those nonprofits that had actually doubled their money, resulted in the profits accrued by the early-stage investors being returned to reduce the losses incurred by the later-stage investors.

Key Lessons

Everybody Likes a Winner

Mr. Bennett was charming and winsome, in spite of his catastrophic, ill-advised, and illegal enterprise. He appeared to be on the inside with big-time philanthropists (creating an illusion of anonymous donors who did not exist), and he proved, over and over again, that he could magically double the money of nonprofits. Until the music stopped, he was a winner, and everybody wanted to be associated with him. Fundraisers are particularly sensitive about connecting with high-wealth individuals and are impressed by others who have made such connections. In the end, a breathtaking array of conservative, solid-thinking individuals and organizations was caught up in being associated with a winner. Every time he doubled the money of another organization, the word-of-mouth support for Mr. Bennett became even stronger.

The Pressure to Raise Funds Can Cloud Judgment

Nonprofit organizations face intense pressure to raise funds. There is no shortage of temptation to find shortcuts. When nonprofit fundraisers, managers, or board members hear amazing stories of peer organizations doubling their money in six months, the temptations increase dramatically. In fact, one might argue that it is irresponsible not to participate, not to double an organization's money in six months, when all of the peer organizations are doing it. The pressure to raise funds in tandem with the success stories of other participating organizations can create a toxic cloud of poor judgment.

Ignore Skeptics at Your Own Peril

Every organization has its naysayers, and they are not universally appreciated. In this case, an astute accounting professor at Spring Arbor College and the cautious president of the Philadelphia Art Museum were lonely voices of skepticism swimming against the tide of enthusiastic support for John Bennett and his unlikely tale of magically doubling nonprofit monies every six months. Imagine calling the authorities to suggest a Ponzi scheme, knowing that hundreds of peers had successfully doubled their money through New Era, earning millions for their respective organizations. Skeptics can be irritatingly persistent and even disruptive. They are not always right. But they are not always wrong. Ignore them at your own peril.

Groupthink Can Be Wrong

The New Era scandal was heightened by the power of groupthink. Powerful word-of-mouth endorsements distributed through established relationships of board members and managers in hundreds of overlapping organizational circles drove New Era's popularity more than sales or promotional efforts. But the groupthink was wrong.

FIVE GREAT QUESTIONS FOR YOUR NEXT BOARD MEETING

1. Do we have adequate policies governing our investments?
2. What steps have our auditors taken or can they take to fully assess and limit our exposure to higher-risk areas?
3. Does our organization's financial management staff have sufficient competency to handle its responsibilities?
4. Are this organization's internal controls adequate?
5. How do we evaluate the antifraud environment in our organization? What steps have we taken to assess our fraud risks?

NOTES

1. "'Religious Fervor' Defense Planned at Fund-Raiser's Fraud Trial,"*New York Times,* March 9, 1997, section 1, p. 1.21.
2. Steve, Stecklow, "Legal Beat: New Era's Bennett Gets 12-Year Sentence,"*Wall Street Journal,* September 23, 1997, section B, p. 15.

3. "Man Accused in Charity Scheme Faces 82 Charges," *New York Times*, September 28, 1996, p. 1.8.
4. Ibid.
5. Steve, Wulf, "Too Good to Be True," *Time*, May 29, 1995.
6. William, Bulkeley, "New Era's Bennett Pleads No Contest," *Wall Street Journal*, March 27, 1997, p. A.
7. Jeff, Jones, "Ex-New Era President Seeks Early Prison Release," *The NonProfit Times*, June 1, 2005.
8. Steve, Stecklow, "New Era's Bennett, Near Sentencing, Tells Judge He Knew Little about Money," *Wall Street Journal*, September 17, 1997, p. 10.
9. "Man Accused in Charity Scheme Faces 82 Charges."
10. William, Power, "Philanthropy: Philadelphia Wonders How It Got Fooled by New Era—and What Lies Ahead," *Wall Street Journal*, May 18, 1995, p. B1.
11. Ibid.
12. Marco, Buscaglia, "College Loses Mega-Bucks on Investment Scam," College Press Service.
13. "Scam Cleanup May Hit Massachusetts Charities, Feds Target Funds from Harvard, MGH, Boston College," *Boston Herald*, January 30, 1996.
14. William, Bulkeley, "Philanthropy: Charities' Coffers Easily Become Crooks' Booty," *Wall Street Journal*, June 5, 1995, p. B1.
15. Ibid.
16. Roger, Lowenstein, "Intrinsic Value: Why Gurus Weren't Wise to New Era's Wiles," *Wall Street Journal*, May 25, 1995, p. C1.
17. Ibid.

CHAPTER 3

Allegheny Health, Education and Research Foundation

TOXIC FAME AND FORTUNE

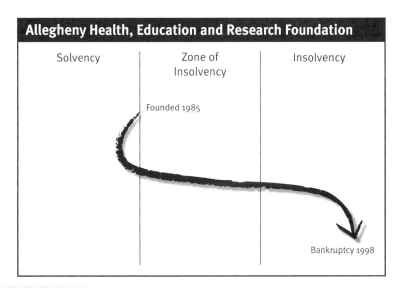

Allegheny Health, Education and Research Foundation

Solvency	Zone of Insolvency	Insolvency
	Founded 1985	Bankruptcy 1998

EXHIBIT 3.1   **ALLEGHENY HEALTH, EDUCATION AND RESEARCH FOUNDATION FINANCIAL PATH**

In December 2002, court documents indicated that Sherif Abdelhak—former president, CEO, and mastermind of the bankrupt $2 billion Allegheny Health, Education and Research Foundation (AHERF), convicted for diverting $52.4 million of donor-restricted contributions from

350 charitable funds to hospital operations—had put his entrepreneurial skills to good use while serving time in a white-collar alternative facility by working his community service hours at a local church where he assisted church leadership in purchasing a building and developing a business plan.[1] AHERF, the largest healthcare system in Pennsylvania, filed for bankruptcy in 1998, with $1.4 billion in debt. Auditor Coopers & Lybrand, which gave AHERF a clean bill of health in the June 1997 audit, was subsequently sued by creditors for $1.5 billion. In May 2000, the Securities and Exchange Commission filed charges against nonprofit healthcare executives for the first time ever, charging David W. McConnell, former chief financial officer for AHERF, and Charles P. Morrison, former chief financial officer for AHERF's Delaware Valley Group, with misleading bond holders by overstating income by $40 million in 1996 and $114 million in 1997.

Sherif Abdelhak, hired as a purchasing coordinator at Allegheny General in 1971, rose to fame and fortune in 25 years, with command over an empire that included 31,000 employees and grossed $2 billion per year (see Exhibit 3.2).

"Perhaps the greatest reported problem was Abdelhak's domination of all board decisions . . ."[2] Board meetings were described as scripted affairs, intentionally staged to limit oversight and participation by other board members. For example, board members (many of whom were busy executives) might receive as many as 1,000 pages of paper to be discussed at board meetings that might last only a short time. As one former member explained, "Half of the people didn't even open the book."[3]

As proof of his domineering style, after acquiring Hahnemann University School of Medicine in 1993, Abdelhak ended his first meeting with the faculty by pointing his finger at them and saying, "Don't cross me or you will live to regret it."[4]

The 1997 filing of the IRS form 990 (Exhibit 3.3) clearly shows mounting losses as indicated by the line 18 deficit of $68,368,424. In April 1998, Abdelhak called in his key executives and demanded that they find ways to cut expenses. Donald Kaye, head of eastern operations, insisted that he must spend money on mandatory repairs to a hospital sprinkler system or he would go to jail. Abdelhak snapped, "Then you'll go to jail. I've done everything for you."[5]

EXHIBIT 3.2   **AHERF BALANCE SHEET**

Allegheny Health, Education and Research Foundation

Balance Sheet: Fiscal Year Ending June 30, 1998

ASSETS	July 1, 1997	June 30, 1998	Change
Cash & Equivalent	$0	$7,130,883	$7,130,883
Accounts Receivable	$15,223,324	$4,624,998	($10,598,326)
Pledges & Grants Receivable	$0	$0	$0
Receivable/Other	$0	$0	$0
Inventories for Sale of Use	$0	$0	$0
Investment/Securities	$225,568,126	$195,055,059	($30,513,067)
Investment/Other	$11,434,779	$11,396,791	($37,988)
Fixed Assets	$34,049,373	$38,074,404	$4,025,031
Other	$148,191,716	$284,387,639	($120,086,212)
Total Assets	**$434,467,318**	**$284,387,639**	**($150,079,679)**
LIABILITIES			
Accounts Payable	$167,402,438	$310,464,532	($36,937,906)
Grants Payable	$0	$0	$0
Deferred Revenue	$716,748	$0	($716,748)
Loans and Notes	$0	$0	$0
Tax-Exempt Bond Liabilities	$0	$0	$0
Other	$105,336,617	$37,614,407	($67,722,210)
Total Liabilities	$273,455,803	$168,078,939	($105,376,864)
Fund Balance	**$161,011,515**	**$116,308,700**	**($44,702,815)**

	12	Total revenue (add lines 1d, 2, 3, 4, 5, 6c, 7, 8d, 9c, 10c, and 11)	12	27,244,129.
Expenses	13	Program services (from line 44, column (B))	13	85,321,161.
	14	Management and general (from line 44, column (C))	14	8,744,129.
	15	Fundraising (from line 44, column (D))	15	1,547,263.
	16	Payments to affiliates (attach schedule)	16	
	17	Total expenses (add lines 16 and 44, column (A))	17	95,612,553.
	18	Excess or (deficit) for the year (subtract line 17 from line 12)	18	-68,368,424.
Net Assets	19	Net assets or fund balances at beginning of year (from line 73, column (A))	19	161,011,515.
	20	Other changes in net assets or fund balances (attach explanation) SEE STATEMENT 2	20	23,665,609.
	21	Net assets or fund balances at end of year (combine lines 18, 19, and 20)	21	116,308,700.

LHA For Paperwork Reduction Act Notice, see page 1 of the separate instructions.   Form 990 (1997)
723001
03-12-98

EXHIBIT 3.3   **AHERF FORM 990 LOSSES**

Under Abdelhak's leadership, salaries and perks skyrocketed, with 77 managers between AHERF's various entities earning in excess of $200,000 per year, while Abdelhak and half a dozen physicians earned in excess of $1 million per year (see Exhibit 3.4). In spite of the considerable salary, the IRS subsequently ruled against Sherif Abdelhak for late filing of 1998

EXHIBIT 3.4   **AHERF LIST OF OFFICERS, TRUSTEES, AND KEY EMPLOYEES COMPENSATION**

Allehgeny Health, Education and Research Foundation

List of Officers, Trustees, and Key Employees

TITLE	COMPENSATION	CONTRIBUTIONS TO BENEFIT PLANS
Pres. & CEO	$777,877	$168,709
Executive VP & Secretary	$792,003	$161,532
Asst Secretary	$108,012	$14,916
Former Pres. & CEO	$1,466,546	$296,846
Executive VP	$1,010,699	$147,555
Treasurer	$436,803	$112,776
Member	$124,998	$17,262
Member	$436,229	$134,188
Former Exec. VP	$887,154	$189,152
Member	$852,068	$242,907
Former Exec. VP	$969,884	$234,838
Member	$436,729	$134,188
Member	$512,279	$129,904
Member	$436,231	$134,189
Asst. Secretary	$77,998	$10,772
Asst. Treasurer	$249,075	$60,300
Member	$274,595	$17,349
Member	$117,325	$16,203
Member	$410,002	$56,621
Member	$524,711	$111,480
Chancellor	$379,446	$99,006
Executive VP	$584,973	$135,046

income taxes and underpayment of $172,626; late filing of 1999 income taxes and underpayment of $31,059; and late filing of his 2000 income taxes with underpayment of $222,655. Perks included private jets, a skybox at Veterans' Stadium, box seats at Three Rivers Stadium, cars, country club memberships, and board meetings in Holland, Switzerland, and Iceland.[6]

One lower-level AHERF administrator wrote, "I still work at a former AHERF facility but will have to work 10 years longer because of the pension plan being $40,000,000 short and the government having to take it over. I am just one person; he (Abdelhak) has ruined many lives. He gave no raises for more than six years while he was giving himself and other executives huge bonuses."[7]

There is no simple explanation for AHERF's journey through the Zone of Insolvency to becoming the largest nonprofit bankruptcy in history. There is no doubt that it was Sherif Abdelhak, CEO, who drove the rapid expansion—purchasing hospitals, physician groups, medical researchers, and medical schools; quadrupling the annual gross revenue, and making AHERF the dominant healthcare system in the state of Pennsylvania. And there is no doubt that he rode roughshod over faculty, employees, executives, and creditors while dominating multiple boards and minimizing their oversight. But this is a story about failure of boards, managers, accountants, auditors, and bond rating regulators. In fact, 10 different boards with no overlapping board memberships governing 55 separate legal entities failed in their fiduciary duties and failed to hold management accountable. They were not prosecuted but had to deal with endless court proceedings, litigation, and public backlash for their role in leading this failed nonprofit into such a massive bankruptcy.

Abdelhak's five-point strategy turned out to be wrong on every point, but it was typical of medical systems strategies of the 1990s. It focused on

1. A statewide integrated system
2. Regional market share to leverage managed care payers
3. Contracts from HMOs to cover all costs of enrollees
4. Achieving synergies among assets
5. Getting referrals from community hospitals to teaching hospitals[8]

Nonprofit boards may experience a number of challenges, such as a ripple effect in the aftermath of the AHERF scandal, according to Orlikoff and Totten.[9] These include

- Increased difficulty in recruiting and retaining board members
- Analysis paralysis, making boards less decisive
- Board focus on regulatory issues thwarting strategic focus
- Reporters and media more antagonistic to boards
- More intrusive state attorneys general
- Directors' and officers' liability insurance more difficult to obtain and more expensive

Jerry Fedele, CEO and president of West Penn Allegheny, made the following statement:[10]

> AHERF was a terrible episode, but I think it was a temporary diversion. Still, a health system doesn't experience turmoil like that without teaching some significant lessons. Those lessons center on governance and leadership. No one person ever had a complete picture of the sprawling system with its dizzying array of corporations and boards of directors. Because of that there was no effective oversight or stewardship and when things started to go bad, you had managers making decisions and guiding it when it should have been the board.

This tragic tale led through the Zone of Insolvency to bankruptcy and dissolution for AHERF, the loss of hundreds of millions of dollars to creditors, the loss of employment and pension funds for thousands, and prison for CEO Sherif Abdelhak. Issues contributing to the collapse of AHERF included a loophole in bylaws that allowed moving cash from donor-restricted funds without donor or board approval, a fragmented governance structure, and financial management silos that were deliberately established to prevent a comprehensive understanding of all of the entities, thereby masking the true financial condition.[11] As with the United Way of America scandal with William Aramony, the news reports focused on issues of style, clouding public understanding of the legal issues.

Key Lessons

A Clean Audit Is No Guarantee

Just one year prior to the bankruptcy, Coopers & Lybrand issued a clean bill of health on the annual audit. Admittedly the firm's judgment was clouded by the fact that the chief financial officer had overstated income by tens of millions of dollars. But even so, losses were accruing and the debt ratio was climbing.

Paying Highest Salary Scale Is No Guarantee

Hiring outstanding talent for high-end health systems is not inexpensive. But Sherif Abdelhak prided himself in paying on the outer edge as a way of recruiting and retaining key executives. If the six- and seven-figure salaries common to AHERF were tied directly to its fiscal success they may have been a justifiable investment. But top-scale pay, given the enterprise's ultimate collapse, appears, in retrospect, both reckless and wasteful. The board left the door open for excess by deferring to management in regard to business details, including executive compensation.

Multiple Corporate Entities Can Mask True Financial Condition

For AHERF and, as we will see in the Baptist Foundation of Arizona, there appears to be a common problem of abuse associated with complex multiple-entity operations. It is far too easy to mask insolvency, excess compensation, debt, and insider trading by manipulating funds through multiple corporations reporting to multiple boards. There are appropriate applications for multiple entities, but board members must take extraordinary care in governing such operations.

Pop Wisdom Is No Guarantee

The expansionist strategy of AHERF was the pop strategy in healthcare circles in the mid-1990s, touted by consultants and experts as the wave of the future. Sherif Abdelhak bought this line, and implemented it with a vengeance, moving aggressively to build the $2 billion enterprise that eventually collapsed. The strategic failure of AHERF must be viewed separately from the criminal misconduct that ensnared key executives. In a fast-paced, hard-charging organization, it can be difficult to argue against the prevailing wisdom.

Board Policies Governing Restricted Funds Are Critical

With over $52 million of donor-restricted funds (i.e., charitable contributions given with specific designations by donors) being raided from AHERF's hospitals, the importance of board policy and the need to monitor board policy come into focus. Unbeknownst to the board, management was manipulating funds between the various entities and using donor-restricted funds to solve cash flow problems. By the time the board had identified the problem and developed a policy, the damage had been inflicted. But even if the proper policies had been in place, monitoring the cash management of donor-restricted funds in multiple entities would have required an extraordinary commitment on the part of the board.

FIVE GREAT QUESTIONS FOR YOUR NEXT BOARD MEETING

1. Do we as a board establish and control our board agendas?
2. Do we really understand the finances of this organization and any related corporations or spin-offs?
3. How do we verify what is reported to us by management?
4. Have we allowed our desire for growth to place this organization in financial distress?
5. What is the correlation between our executive compensation plan and organizational outcomes?

■ NOTES

1. Arthur, Lazarus, "The Aftermath of AHERF: Keeping Your Career Afloat," *Physician Executive*, vol. 32, Issue 3 (2006): 20–24.
2. Lawton, Burns, John Cacciamani, James Clement, and Welman Aquino, "The Fall of the House of AHERF: The Allegheny Bankruptcy," *Health Affairs*, January–February 2000.
3. Ibid.
4. Lazarus, "The Aftermath of AHERF."
5. Steve, Massey, "Anatomy of a Bankruptcy Part 1: Wake Up to Break Up," *The Post Gazette,* January 17, 1999.
6. Ibid.
7. Lazarus, "The Aftermath of AHERF."
8. "The Patient Died: A Post-mortem on America's Largest Nonprofit Healthcare Failure," Knowledge@Wharton, January 20, 2000.
9. Orlikoff, James E., and Mary K. Totten, "Effective Governance After Enron and AHERF," *Trustee Magazine*, vol. 55 Issue 7, (July–August 2002), p. W1.
10. Becker, Cinda, "AHERF Revisited," *Modern Healthcare*, vol. 35, Issue 26, June 27, 2005, p. 40.
11. Ibid.

CHAPTER 4

National Alliance of Business

PROACTIVE IN CLOSURE

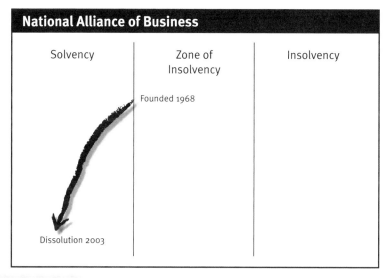

National Alliance of Business

| Solvency | Zone of Insolvency | Insolvency |

Founded 1968

Dissolution 2003

EXHIBIT 4.1   NATIONAL ALLIANCE OF BUSINESS ZONE
FINANCIAL PATH

In 2003, the National Alliance of Business (NAB) closed its doors after 35 years of service. NAB rose out of the poverty programs of the 1960s, founded by President Lyndon B. Johnson and Henry Ford II, focused on workforce development for youth and adults in poverty. In the early years, NAB was fully funded by the U.S. Department of Labor (DOL), with national, regional, and major metro offices staffed by loaned business executives committed to training and hiring unemployed poor youth and adults (see Exhibit 4.1).

Roberts T. Jones served as president and chief executive officer of the National Alliance of Business and initiated discussions with the board that lead to the decision to cease operations. Prior to his tenure at NAB, Jones had served as vice president of RJR Nabisco, Inc. and subsequently served as assistant secretary of labor for both Presidents Reagan and George H. W. Bush. He has also served on the Board of Overseers of the Malcolm Baldridge National Quality Award, the Board of Trustees of the Carnegie Foundation for the Advancement of Teaching, and the boards of American College Testing, the Management and Training Corporation, the Career Training Foundation, and the Talent Alliance. He is coauthor of a book, *The Jobs Revolution: Changing How America Works*.[1] Jones understands corporate management and governance, both for-profit and nonprofit, and has demonstrated a lifelong passion for the importance of education and training for workforce development.

Roberts T. Jones was instrumental in moving the Malcolm Baldridge process, used initially to spur quality management in business, into the public school arena. A spokesman for NAB said, "While random acts of improvement can boost school performance, it is only when those changes are properly aligned in a strategic plan that major long-term results emerge."[2] Through NAB, the business community increasingly focused on the need to improve the quality of public schools, recognizing that this would require an investment, pay incentives, and performance measurement systems similar to those used in business. Pay for performance—rather than the traditional public school salary scale that pays based on experience and education—might be critical to inspiring high-quality educators for the future. "Many teachers feel they're at the bottom of the hill and everybody's standing on the top of the hill rolling rocks at them," said NAB chairman Keith Bailey, president and CEO of Williams Corporation. "It won't be unusual to see [some] teachers in a school making $100,000 a year," Jones predicted.[3]

President Ronald Reagan clearly articulated the importance of the mission in a speech at the NAB's annual meeting at the Washington Sheraton on October 5, 1981 when he stated,

> [T]he National Alliance of Business was formed to reduce the despair of unemployment, to provide opportunities where they would otherwise

not exist. You've set for yourselves a noble and necessary goal. You know that a job at $4 an hour is priceless in terms of the self-respect it can buy. Many people today are economically trapped in welfare. They'd like nothing better than to be out in the work-a-day world with the rest of us. Independence and self-sufficiency is what they want. They aren't lazy or unwilling to work; they just don't know how to free themselves from that welfare security blanket.

Under Jones's leadership, NAB escalated its commitment to focus public attention on improving the education system, involving the captains of industry in the nationwide quest to train a knowledge-based workforce critical to the success of American businesses. In 2001, NAB honored the president and CEO of Intel, Dr. Craig R. Barrett, with the prestigious Founder's Award in recognition of his leadership and Intel's contributions in excess of $100 million annually to raise the performance of America's students. Barrett stated,

> The economy of the future depends on the quality of our schools and the ability of our students to compete. We need to provide our public schools with what business brings to the table: our emphasis on setting goals, measuring results, and getting things done. And that means getting involved in policy decisions because public policies on education are every bit as important to us as policies on employment, technology or trade.[4]

NAB served millions of people over three decades by providing workplace training to move them from dependence to independence. After being fully funded by the DOL, NAB had transitioned in the 1980s to a business model combining contract revenue from DOL with corporate sponsorship. By the year 2000, federal funding was totally eliminated and NAB was totally dependent on its own fundraising initiatives through dues, sponsorships of its 5,000 members, and grants from private foundations.

By 2003, Jones concluded that the work of NAB, as originally envisioned, was complete. The market had changed, new issues had emerged, and new organizations had risen to the challenge. Funding sources had changed, and the organization experienced some net losses, as demonstrated in Exhibit 4.2. It still had net assets, however, although they were starting to dwindle, as shown in Exhibit 4.3. Boldly Jones encouraged the board members to consider their work complete, celebrate their success, and

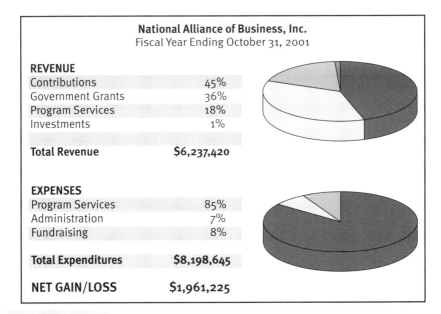

National Alliance of Business, Inc.
Fiscal Year Ending October 31, 2001

REVENUE

Contributions	45%
Government Grants	36%
Program Services	18%
Investments	1%
Total Revenue	**$6,237,420**

EXPENSES

Program Services	85%
Administration	7%
Fundraising	8%
Total Expenditures	**$8,198,645**
NET GAIN/LOSS	**$1,961,225**

EXHIBIT 4.2   **NAB REVENUES AND EXPENSES**

SOURCE: GuideStar, www.guidestar.org.

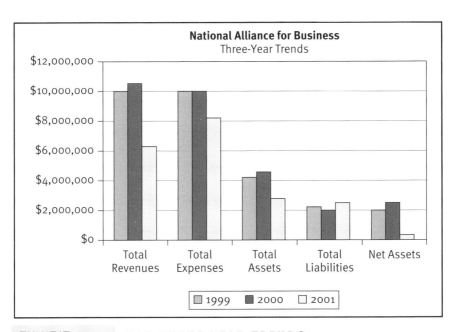

EXHIBIT 4.3   **NAB THREE-YEAR TRENDS**

cease operations. Within three months, the deliberations were complete and the closedown began.

Roberts T. Jones made the following statement:

> I believe there is often a disconnect between the day a nonprofit is chartered and the years of experience that follow. . . . [O]ver time the boards shift from people who are connected to a purpose driven charter, to people who are simply honored to be there. Granting a nonprofit charter to a new organization ought to be a tougher process requiring annual achievement of key benchmarks. Nonprofit organizations, when incorporated, should, in essence, be granted a license to operate for a set purpose and period of time, then sunset.

Nobody joins a nonprofit board to close the organization down. Typically, nonprofit board members are unpaid volunteers, committed to the cause and eager to help. Discussion of dissolution quickly brings a myriad of emotions to the surface. "Am I being disloyal to the mission and history of this organization because I am considering dissolution?" And for one board member who does not feel guilty enough based on introspection, there is most likely another board member or manager who will heap on the feelings of guilt. "If you really feel that the organization should close, obviously you are not passionate about the mission and should just resign from the board."

This is a tale of an organization that served well and made the decision to close without traveling through the Zone of Insolvency. The dissolution was driven by environmental change, not by legal or ethical issues. Performance ratios were shifting due to changes in funding, as evidenced by decreases in the program ratio and increases in the debt ratio (see Exhibit 4.4). Net assets were dwindling, a possible indicator of future business viability (see Exhibit 4.5) in comparison with peer organizations. NAB was proactive in closure, opting to close the books with net assets still remaining. One could argue that the need to improve the education system for workforce development still exists, and it does. But the world changed radically between 1968 and 2003, impacting NAB's ability to sustain funding and cost-effectively address the mission. A great organization serving a real and ongoing need closed its doors out of a strong conviction that the time had come for other organizations, more effectively positioned for the future, to carry the ball.

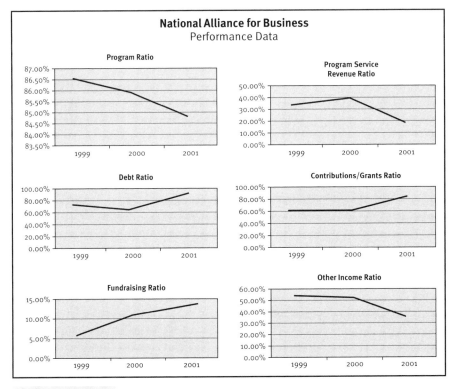

EXHIBIT 4.4   NAB PERFORMANCE DATA

SOURCE: GuideStar, www.guidestar.com.

Key Lessons

Organizations Have Life Cycles

The average Fortune 500 company lasts just 40 years. There is nothing to say that a nonprofit should last forever. Organizations have life cycles, and it is critical to know where your organization stands. Perhaps it is a rising star, perhaps it is maturing, or perhaps it is nearing the end of its productive life. Artificially sustaining the nonprofit organization is not a legal or ethical requirement of a board. In fact, there may be legal or ethical justifications for dissolution.

There Is No Inherent Dishonor in Dissolution

The accomplishments of NAB are in no way diminished by its dissolution. This is an organization that had a significant impact on public policy for

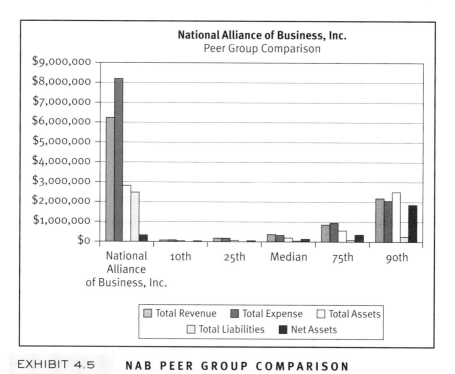

EXHIBIT 4.5   **NAB PEER GROUP COMPARISON**

SOURCE: GuideStar, www.guidestar.com.

decades. Millions of young people and adults in poverty found training and employment, thanks to the good work of NAB. In this case, the board understood and respected the history; it also understood that the environment had changed and that the baton needed to be passed to other organizations that could more effectively address the issues of the future.

FIVE GREAT QUESTIONS FOR YOUR NEXT BOARD MEETING

1. How has the environment changed since our founding, and how does that impact our future?
2. Are we positioned to continue effectively serving our mission in the future?
3. Is it possible that we should celebrate our success and pass the baton to others?

4. Have we established a threshold of minimum net assets and agreed that dropping below the minimum would trigger a filing for dissolution?

5. Are we continuing this organization by default or by design?

Notes

1. Also authored by Steven Gunderson, Robert Jones, Kathryn Scanland, published by Copywriters Inc. in 2004.
2. Broder, David, "Good Business in the Schools," *Washington Post*, July 14, 1999, section A, p. 23.
3. Ibid.
4. "National Alliance of Business Honors Intel CEO for Contributions to Public Education; Craig Barrettt Urges Business to Make Education as High a Priority as Labor and Technology Policy," *Business Wire*, November 6, 2001.

CHAPTER 5

United Way National Capital Area

RIGHTS OF OWNERSHIP

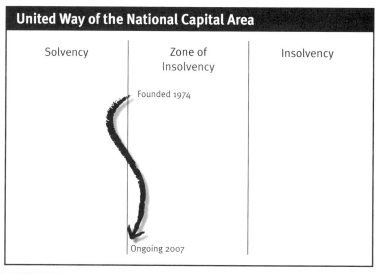

United Way of the National Capital Area

Solvency | Zone of Insolvency | Insolvency

Founded 1974

Ongoing 2007

EXHIBIT 5.1   UNITED WAY OF THE NATIONAL CAPITAL AREA FINANCIAL PATH

In March 2004, Oral Suer, president of the United Way of the National Capital Area (UWNCA), pleaded guilty to transporting stolen money across state lines; making false statements and concealing facts relating to an employee pension plan; and defrauding the United Way of almost $500,000 for bowling, trips to Las Vegas, enhancements to his pension contributions, and payment to himself for annual leave.[1] The judge subsequently sentenced Suer to 27 months in prison plus $497,000 in restitution. Not satisfied with the settlement, officials at the United Way filed a civil suit demanding restitution of $1.6 million. An August 2004 audit report by PricewaterhouseCoopers stated that the UWNCA executive received $2.4 million more than his approved compensation between 1974 and 2002.[2] Suer is not a U.S. citizen and does not have permanent resident status. It is anticipated that he will be deported to Turkey after serving his prison time (see Exhibit 5.1).[3]

UWNCA was founded in 1974 through a merger of the United Givers Fund, the Health and Welfare Council, and the United Black Fund. One of the largest of the United Way's 1,400 local campaigns, it raises funds for over 900 local nonprofits annually. UWNCA touts many success stories of individual lives impacted, such as an alcoholic named John, who was helped by rehab, job training, and employment; Cinnamon, who was homeless six years ago but today at age 23 is a college graduate and homeowner; and Mun Tan Lee, an immigrant from South Korea, who was helped with English literacy skills.

Suer left a huge blemish on the good work of UWNCA by borrowing a page from the United Way's Aramony scandal and traveling down the same path. After building assets through years of net gains, as shown in Exhibit 5.2, UWNCA experienced a dramatic increase in debt and decreases in contributions immediately following the scandal, as displayed in Exhibit 5.3. Even so, running the United Way of the National Capital Area for 29 years, Suer acted as though the funds were for his own personal benefit, treating himself to perks that were not his to award. Nonprofit executives and their boards must guard against the tendency for longtime executives to assume the role of owners, in violation of the nonprofit charter. This insidious path can seem benign at the start, but over time can lead to a pattern of material violations of fiscal trust. Evidence seems to suggest that Suer's abuses trace back to 1976. Abuses can be issues of style that simply offend the sensibilities of donors and sponsors, or in fact can be violations of the law, with criminal implications. Arguably, the owner of a small for-profit business has more latitude with legally allowable perks and expenses than are appropriate or acceptable in the nonprofit arena. In the case of UWNCA, there were significant issues of fraud and embezzlement.

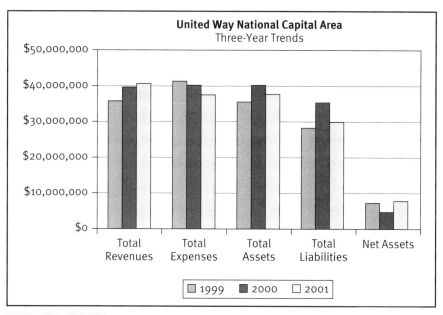

EXHIBIT 5.2   **UWNCA THREE-YEAR TRENDS**

SOURCE: GuideStar, www.guidestar.com.

"We are shocked and outraged by the findings of the audit released this morning," said William Couper, chair of the UWNCA board. "The United Way and the community it serves were abused."[4]

"This is a story about greed and the violation of trust," said U.S. Attorney Paul J. McNulty. "Mr. Suer treated the charity like his personal ATM."[5]

According to the PricewaterhouseCoopers audit report,

> Mr. Suer on a number of occasions made payment of his own personal pledges to UWNCA campaigns via UWNCA advances requested by him and paid to him. By 2001, after years of siphoning off cash at every turn, Suer had cultivated a help-yourself-and-hide-the-details culture. Some employees took reimbursements for the tax liability they accrued for personal use of United Way cars. They cashed personal checks and had the finance department hold them until they had money to cover them, a short-term loan by any name.[6]

Reports of the scandal drew an immediate and prolonged response from individual donors and corporate sponsors. Charitable gifts dropped

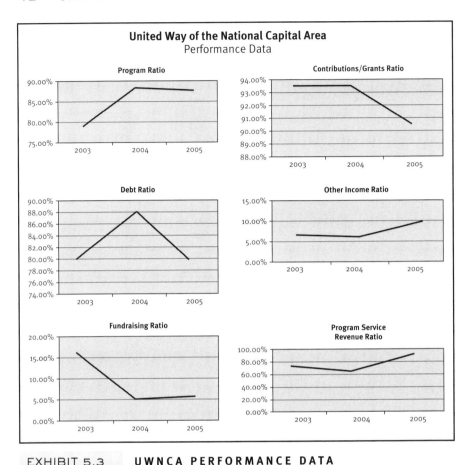

EXHIBIT 5.3   UWNCA PERFORMANCE DATA

SOURCE: GuideStar, www.guidestar.com.

from over $90 million per year to less than $40 million per year, and UWNCA was forced to reduce staff from 90 to 35. Major corporate sponsor, the Washington Redskins, chose to sit out the campaign after news of the scandal, followed by numerous other sponsors who felt obligated to refrain until they were assured that their funds were being appropriately managed. In an effort to deal head-on with public concerns about the integrity of UWNCA, the organization developed the following accountability statement:

> United Way's mission is to create progressive change and positive results in our local communities through effective, efficient, and ethical

fundraising. To succeed in this mission, we have revolutionized the way we do business, and renewed our dedication to open, accountable, outcome-oriented management.

Leading With Integrity

- New, fully committed management
- Smaller, vigilant, more engaged 21 member board for greater oversight
- Code of Conduct, adopted and signed by all staff and volunteers
- Appointment of an independent ethics officer

Managing Responsibility

- Tightened financial policies controls, including a ban on employee contracts
- Tough internal open-ended audit of our past and a goal of seeking restitution for the community
- Flat 12.5% fundraising and administrative fee
- Streamlined organization, plus a significantly reduced operating budget

Focusing on Impact

- Active listening and partnering to identify and address critical needs
- Monthly funding for agencies, giving them more budget certainty
- Moratorium on admission of new agencies while campaign eligibility standards are aligned with the direction of the organization

Chuck Anderson stepped into UWNCA as the new CEO in August 2003, just weeks before the release of the audit report. During the job interview, the board asked him how he would share the upcoming bad news audit report with the public. "I'd take that sucker and put it right on the Web," said Anderson. "Let the whole world read the good, the bad, and the ugly about this organization."[7]

This tale meandered into the Zone of Insolvency and back out to fiscal viability. In the process, the CEO was fired, fined, and sentenced to prison; all board members were required to resign to make room for an entirely new board; and more than half of the staff was terminated. Total charitable gifts and sponsorships plummeted during and immediately after the scandal, creating financial hardship for dozens of funded organizations. Legal fees exceeded $1 million, and hundreds of thousands of dollars were spent on public relations efforts to restore fundraising productivity. The Washington Redskins withdrew their long-standing endorsement. And later, in 2006, with UWNCA still trying to dig out from the public distrust caused by the Suer scandal, the chief financial officer resigned in frustration over issues of financial reporting on funds raised.

Key Lessons

Donors Vote with Their Checkbooks

Donors vote very effectively with their checkbooks, demonstrating or withdrawing support. In the case of UWNCA, donors immediately lost confidence and withheld tens of millions of dollars. Fundraising, above all else, is based on trust, and once that trust is violated, donors can have very long memories.

Familiarity Breeds Contempt

Oral Suer siphoned money out of the UWNCA over a span of three decades, and the longer he stayed, the more free he felt to use the organization for his own personal benefit. Worse yet, he bred a culture of lax internal controls, and other employees found their own ways to benefit personally at the expense of the organization. It appears that Suer had a fundamental attitude of entitlement even in his early years that grew more pronounced with time, leading to more egregious abuses.

Trust Is Not an Excuse for Accountability

Good governance calls for appropriate accountability. The board is to hold the chief executive accountable. The chief executive is to hold his direct reports accountable, and so on down through the ranks of employees. It is not acceptable to go easy on the accountability factors just because "you trust." The old cliché, "Don't expect what you don't inspect," holds true. Boards cannot afford to be shy or lax about the accountability issues, regardless of the affinity they feel or the degree of trust they place in the chief executive.

FIVE GREAT QUESTIONS FOR YOUR NEXT BOARD MEETING

1. Does this board have an executive compensation committee with appropriate policies and internal controls?
2. Does this board have a policy that requires any reports of financial discrepancies to be reported to the full board?
3. Who approves all expense reimbursements of our CEO?
4. Do we have an audit commit separate and independent from the finance committee?
5. Are we as a board balancing our trust in our CEO with a prudent measure of accountability?

NOTES

1. Jacqueline, Salmon, "Area United Way's Ex-Chief Admits $500,000 Fraud," *Washington Post,* March 5, 2004, section B, p. 1.
2. Ian, Wilhelm and Brad Wolverton, "DC United Way Executive Pleads Guilty to Stealing $500,000," *The Chronicle of Philanthropy,* March 4, 2004.
3. Jerry, Markon, "Ex-Chief of Local United Way Sentenced," *Washington Post,* May, 2004 15, section A, p. 1.
4. Amelia, Gruber, "Capital Area United Way Mishandled CFC Funds, Auditors Find," *Government Executive,* August 12, 2003.
5. Wilhelm and Wolverton, "DC United Way Executive Pleads Guilty to Stealing $500,000."
6. Bill, Birchard, "Nonprofits by the Numbers," National Council of Nonprofit Associations, July 2005.
7. Ibid.

CHAPTER 6

Baptist Foundation of Arizona

TOO GOOD TO BE TRUE (ACT II)

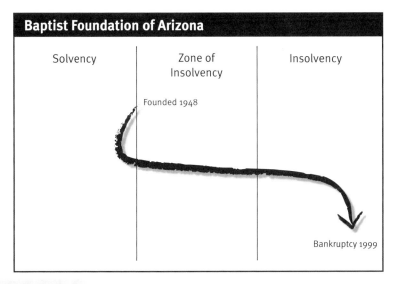

Baptist Foundation of Arizona

| Solvency | Zone of Insolvency | Insolvency |

Founded 1948

Bankruptcy 1999

EXHIBIT 6.1   BAPTIST FOUNDATION OF ARIZONA FINANCIAL PATH

In September 2006, William P. Crotts, an attorney and former president of the Baptist Foundation of Arizona (BFA), was sentenced to eight years in prison, and Thomas D. Grabinski, former chief counsel of the foundation, was sentenced to six years for fraud and conducting of an illegal enterprise. They were each ordered to pay restitution of $159 million[1] and were led from the courtroom in handcuffs. This concluded a 10-month trial that documented a complex, $600 million Ponzi scheme, featuring Bible-quoting salesmen selling retirement investments to church members at above-market rates. Arthur Andersen, having provided "clean" audit opinions on the foundation's financial statements from 1984 to 1997, subsequently settled a suit by the foundation for $217 million without admitting or denying any fault (see Exhibit 6.1). A pastor who blew the whistle early and suggested that the foundation had defrauded him of $100,000 received death threats, found the words "white trash" painted on his house, and had half of his congregation withdraw their church membership. "The majority of Southern Baptist victims in the courtroom wore white ribbons in support of Crotts and Grabinski, depicting them as humble Christians and excellent family men who would never intentionally break the law."[2]

This chapter 11 bankruptcy filing represents the largest nonprofit filing on record. The $217 million settlement from Arthur Andersen was by far the largest payout ever made by Andersen, but it was shortly thereafter dwarfed as a result of Andersen's involvement in Enron. (In fact, the same month that Arthur Andersen settled with the bankruptcy trustee for the Baptist Foundation, Andersen also offered to pay $750 million to settle with Enron, an offer that was immediately rejected by attorneys for Enron.) In addition to the settlement paid by Andersen, BFA legal counsel Jennings Strouss & Salmon PLC paid a $21 million settlement in regard to its role in the failure of the foundation. Unfortunately, it was not the auditors, the accountants, or the board that brought the fraud to light, but rather a series of articles in a Phoenix newspaper.

Linda Rizer, a spokesperson for Arthur Andersen, proudly stated that the auditor's job is not to find fraud. "We were hired to make sure their books balanced," said Rizer.[3] Arthur Andersen argued that the board and managers of the foundation withheld critical information from auditors to mask the true situation.

"Just once, it would be nice if one of the Big Five accounting firms actually showed remorse for the suffering that investors have had to go through," said Lynn Turner, a former chief accountant for the Securities and Exchange Commission. On review, the State Board of Accountancy identified material departures from generally accepted accounting principles and indicated that Andersen should have issued either qualified or adverse opinions for fiscal years 1991 to 1994.[4] professor Roman Weil, calculating damages for the liquidating trustee, demonstrated that because the foundation continued in operation after the point that auditors should have identified the insolvency, BFA lost assets in excess of $150 million that could have been used to pay the claims of creditors.[5]

The astounding pace of growth in Baptist Foundation sales of retirement securities was fueled by suggestions of return rates that were simply too good to be true. Due, in part, to the brand affiliation with the Southern Baptist denomination, church members threw caution to the winds and rushed to invest their lifetime savings and retirement funds with the Baptist Foundation of Arizona. Commenting on this massive fraud and its 11,000 churchgoing victims, the president of the North American Association of Securities Administrators noted that church-based affinity fraud is a growing challenge for regulators.[6]

In the mid-1980s, the foundation acted on a major strategic shift and began investing heavily in Arizona real estate, including a geographically misplaced purchase of an 82-acre resort on the Big Island of Hawaii, while pushing IRA-type investment plans for elderly church members. Marketing and sales materials touted the safety of these investments and assured potential investors that no investor had ever lost a penny on foundation investments. The IRA-style investments skyrocketed from $7,000 in 1984 to over $200 million in 1985, but then the real estate market began to cool off. Determined not to show losses, as illustrated in Exhibit 6.2, management established over 90 independent corporations closely held by friends and affiliates of the foundation, selling properties back and forth while recording receivables at book value instead of current (depreciated market) value. Hiding losses of over $20 million per year, management paid interest to investors out of the principal of new investors, using the classic Ponzi scheme.[7] In July 1999, the Securities Division of the Arizona Corporation Commission officially notified the Baptist Foundation of Arizona that it was not properly informing investors of the true financial condition of the corporation. By August, the foundation agreed to a cease-and-desist order, which halted all new income from investors. By November 1999, without inflow of new investor dollars, the Ponzi scheme collapsed under its own weight, and the foundation filed for bankruptcy.

The foundation's 11,000 investor victims were soon deluged with letters from attorneys seeking to represent them in the bankruptcy hearings. Ultimately, the victims were organized in a class action suit, and the

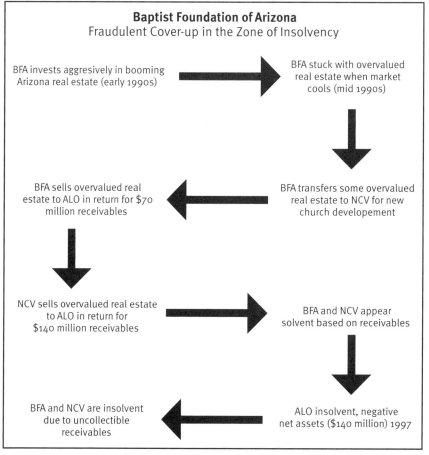

Baptist Foundation of Arizona
Fraudulent Cover-up in the Zone of Insolvency

BFA invests aggresively in booming Arizona real estate (early 1990s) → BFA stuck with overvalued real estate when market cools (mid 1990s)

BFA sells overvalued real estate to ALO in return for $70 million receivables ← BFA transfers some overvalued real estate to NCV for new church developement

NCV sells overvalued real estate to ALO in return for $140 million receivables → BFA and NCV appear solvent based on receivables

BFA and NCV are insolvent due to uncollectible receivables ← ALO insolvent, negative net assets ($140 million) 1997

EXHIBIT 6.2   **BFA FRAUDULENT COVER-UP IN THE ZONE OF INSOLVENCY**

bankruptcy trustee was able to manage the dissolution, liquidate remaining assets, and return to victims approximately 73 cents on every dollar invested. Regulators appointed an outside panel of experts to monitor professional standards at Arthur Andersen's Phoenix office, and two of the key Andersen partners involved with the foundation account were stripped of their CPA credentials.

Eighty-year-old Darrell Tramel and his wife, June, lost their lifetime savings of $1.2 million eventually recovering about three-quarters of that. While waiting on the bankruptcy trustee to complete the liquidation and return recovered funds, Mr. Tramel took a job selling candy in a mall, and Mrs. Tramel took a job in a pet store to try to make ends meet. "You have given Southern Baptists a bad name," said Mr. Tramel to the Baptist Foundation executives during the trial.[8]

Board members, volunteers, and benefactors of nonprofit organizations often underestimate the potential liabilities of their activities. Note that the bankruptcy trustee alleged wrongdoing by the following six parties, negotiated with these parties to waive their claim of $37 million against BFA, and required them to pay a combined total of $16.5 million. The parties involved were

1. L. Dwain Hoover and Affiliates, for breach of fiduciary responsibility as board member, and for transactions with BFA not kept at arm's length, which subsequently contributed to financial collapse. Hoover was alleged to owe the foundation over $11 million.[9]
2. Harold Friend and Affiliates, who alleged to be a benefactor of BFA but who, in fact, facilitated the fraud through certain transactions with BFA. Friend, a former BFA board member, was alleged to have borrowed over $2 million from the foundation.[10]
3. Edgar Alan Kuhn, for perpetuating fraud through his role in EVIG, an entity controlled by BFA and used to conceal losses.
4. Jalma Hunsinger and Affiliates, for his role in ALO, a BFA-controlled entity used to perpetuate the fraud and hide losses through bogus sales. Hunsinger was alleged to owe the foundation over $120 million.[11]
5. Arizona Southern Baptist Convention, for failure to exercise its fiduciary responsibility through its seat on the board of BFA, and for failing to take a more active role in detecting and halting the fraud.
6. Nelson Lambson and Henry & Horne, for malpractice when their law firms failed to discover that BFA had not complied with relevant IRS regulations to serve as a non-bank passive custodian of individual retirement accounts.

This tale wound through the Zone of Insolvency to bankruptcy, dissolution, lawsuits against the accounting firm and the law firm, loss of retirement funds for 11,000 of Arizona's elderly, a tarnished image for the denomination, prison terms for the CEO and CFO, and multimillion-dollar claims against board members and former board members. Amazingly, as shown in the July 2006 letter from the Office of the Attorney General (see Exhibit 6.3), the State of Arizona has "limited jurisdiction, if any,

Terry Goddard
Attorney General

Office of the **Attorney General**
State of Arizona

James P. Walsh
Chief Deputy Attorney General
Direct Line: 602.542.7711
Direct Fax: 602.542.1964

July 27, 2006

Ron Mattocks
President
Mattocks & Associates, Inc.
12611 Lake Normandy Lane
Fairfax, VA 22030

Re: Not-for-Profit Corporations in the Zone of Insolvency

Dear Mr. Mattocks:

Attorney General Goddard has asked me to respond to your July 5 letter. As I understand it, you are doing research for a book on non-profits. The Attorney General of Arizona has very limited jurisdiction, if any, over non-profits. Thus, the questions you ask are not those for which information is readily available to our Office.

We do think that the non-profit sector is an important sector to monitor. We would be interested in the results of your research project.

I regret that we are unable to help you with the information you seek. I wish you the best in your efforts.

Sincerely yours,

James P. Walsh
Chief Deputy Attorney General

1275 West Washington, Phoenix, Arizona 85007-2926 • Phone 602.542.4266 • Fax 602.542.4085

EXHIBIT 6.3   **LETTER FROM THE OFFICE OF THE ATTORNEY GENERAL**

over non-profits," in spite of being the home state to this massive Ponzi scheme. The Southern Baptist Theological Seminary distanced itself from the foundation and from the Southern Baptist Convention, as did Grand Canyon University, another Southern Baptist school, in legal maneuvers designed to avoid liabilities for the deficit. A grassroots group called "Restoring Our Integrity" asked that each of Arizona's 400 Southern Baptist churches contribute 1% of their undesignated gift receipts to restore the foundation, but found that only a minority of churches was willing to participate.

Key Lessons

Spin-off Corporations

By the time of its collapse, BFA had spun out over 90 related entities in a complex web designed to cover up losses that would have revealed the true insolvency. How could the board's members not have been aware of the existence of these corporations? And if they were aware, how could they not be concerned about such a convoluted scheme? And why did numerous past board members feel so free to step in and help create these shell corporations that masked the insolvency from auditors and investors?

Multitiered Governance Structures Hide Problems

The Baptist Foundation of Arizona was affiliated with the Southern Baptist Convention. This gave BFA instant recognition and affinity with Arizona's 400 Southern Baptist churches. Parishioners had a level of confidence inherent in this affiliation and were even more inclined to invest when told that their investments would somehow benefit the denomination and its causes. But the Southern Baptist Convention felt that it had minimal control of or responsibility for BFA by virtue of its one board seat.

Be Wary of Insider Transactions

The level of insider transactions, with hundreds of millions of dollars of loans, purchases, and sales involving board members and past board members, was absolutely breathtaking. The scope of the claims against these insiders, negotiated by the bankruptcy trustee for out-of-court settlements, established the true level of the misconduct. It is difficult to imagine how board members who were not alleged to have been part of the insider transactions could have been exercising their fiduciary responsibilities while remaining totally unaware of the insider trading.

Evaluate Receivables with Skepticism

The foundation balance sheets carried hundreds of millions of dollars of receivables, known by the board to be primarily real estate investments. Given that the real estate market was significantly depressed, the board's lack of skepticism about the viability of the receivables is puzzling to say the least. Even a modest level of inquisitiveness by board, accountants, or auditors regarding receivables would have lead to a better understanding of the multiple spin-off entities and insider trading, along with an understanding that the inflated sales prices had created insolvent spin-offs and uncollectible receivables.

Realistic Expectations of Auditors

The prudent board will not rely totally on the auditors to ferret out wrongdoers. Every audit letter reiterates that the auditors rely on truthful representations by management. Clearly there was enough blame to go around here, as evidenced by claims against Andersen and individual board members. But a board member who disengages and trusts that if there are financial improprieties they will be found by the auditors is at risk of failing to fulfill his or her basic fiduciary responsibility, and potentially becoming liable for misinformed decisions or lack of prudence while operating in the Zone of Insolvency.

FIVE GREAT QUESTIONS FOR YOUR NEXT BOARD MEETING

1. Do we have adequate conflict-of-interest policies to prevent insider trading?
2. Do we monitor for insider trading by board or management?
3. Do we as a board have appropriate concern for the collectability of receivables listed on the balance sheet?

4. Do we have spin-off entities that may mask the true nature of our finances?
5. Are we as a board working appropriately with our auditors to reduce the likelihood of fraud, embezzlement, or other criminal behavior?

Notes

1. Terry Greene, Sterling, "Executives Sentenced in Church Fraud; Investors Lost Millions to Southern Baptist Foundation Scheme in Arizona," *Washington Post,* October 1, 2006, section A, p. 8.
2. Lawrence, Mohrweis, "Lessons from the Baptists Foundation Fraud," *The CPA Journal,* vol. 73, issue 7 (2003) p. 50.
3. David S., Hilzenrath, "Two Failures with a Familiar Ring: Arthur Andersen Audited Foundation, S&L That Collapsed," *Washington Post,* December 6, 2001, section A, p. 21.
4. Mohrweis, "Lessons from the Baptists Foundation Fraud."
5. *Baptist Foundation of Arizona v. Arthur Andersen,* The Analysis Group, 2007.
6. Mohrweis, "Lessons from the Baptists Foundation Fraud."
7. Ibid.
8. Sterling, "Executives Sentenced in Church Fraud."
9. Terry Greene, Sterling, "The Money Changers: A New Times Investigation," *The Phoenix New Times,* April 16, 1998.
10. Ibid.
11. Ibid.

CHAPTER 7

Western Fairfax Christian Ministries

FAITH VERSUS PRUDENCE

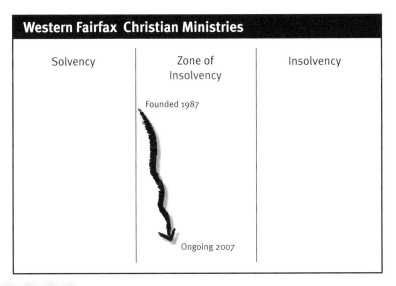

Western Fairfax Christian Ministries

Solvency | Zone of Insolvency | Insolvency

Founded 1987

Ongoing 2007

EXHIBIT 7.1   WESTERN FAIRFAX CHRISTIAN MINISTRIES FINANCIAL PATH

In March 2007, staff and supporters of Western Fairfax Christian Ministries (WFCM) marched into a Fairfax County, Virginia, Board of Supervisors meeting immediately before the vote on the budget for the new fiscal year, carrying banners and demanding that the county bail them out of their financial distress with a $120,000 grant (see Exhibit 7.1). Founded in 1987, WFCM provides food, clothing, and shelter to families in financial crisis, helping them to get back on their feet and avoid homelessness.

County Board of Supervisors chairman Gerald E. Connolly was surprised by the demands and declined an immediate bailout, stating, "[T]hey have not been willing to commit to reforms that would provide transparency and accountability. We can't be using taxpayer dollars to bail out an organization that the county does not consider competent." Ironically, in a desperate attempt to avoid eviction due to unpaid rent, WFCM, the organization that helps families in financial crisis avoid eviction, cut its own budget by over 50% and terminated most of the staff.[1] Sully district supervisor Michael Frey was hopeful that the organization would stay in business, but said, "It is not the first nonprofit to be in business difficulties."[2]

WFCM was formed as a coalition of churches to more efficiently serve people in Fairfax County who were unable to meet the basic human needs of food, clothing, and shelter. In 2004, in an effort to address the rapidly escalating needs for public assistance in the county, the organization relocated, obtaining more space for operations, but increasing the monthly rental costs by 900%. This led to net losses within two years, as shown in Exhibit 7.2. The new noncancellable five-year lease at the cost of $87,300 per year represented a total five-year obligation of $436,500. Rapid expansion of staffing, program expenses, and the new lease payments exceeded WFCM's sustainable fundraising capacity, driving the organization into financial distress. As the debt ratio increased, the program ratio decreased, as shown in Exhibit 7.3. In May 2007, with WFCM three months in arrears on rent payments and threatening to file for dissolution, the landlord agreed to a three-month reprieve while the organization sorted out its funding.

Ending homelessness is more cost-effective than managing it. WFCM spent an estimated $16,000 in case management per family assisted in 2006. During 2007, the organization experienced a 67% increase in requests for assistance from its food pantry for the needy. The cost of public assistance for a family that has lost its home can easily climb to $100,000 or more. Over 80% of the people that turn to WFCM for assistance are employed but not making enough money to live in Fairfax County. The National Alliance to End Homelessness estimates that the average cost of placing the children of a homeless family into foster care

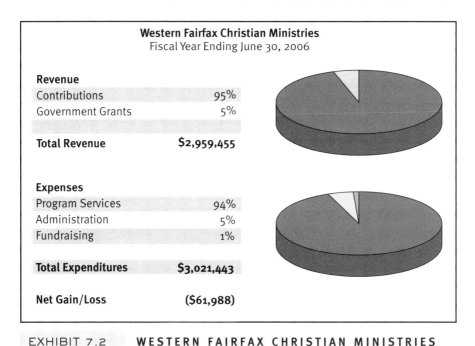

Western Fairfax Christian Ministries
Fiscal Year Ending June 30, 2006

Revenue

Contributions	95%
Government Grants	5%
Total Revenue	**$2,959,455**

Expenses

Program Services	94%
Administration	5%
Fundraising	1%
Total Expenditures	**$3,021,443**
Net Gain/Loss	**($61,988)**

EXHIBIT 7.2   WESTERN FAIRFAX CHRISTIAN MINISTRIES
REVENUES AND EXPENSES

SOURCE: GuideStar, www.guidestar.com.

is over $47,000, compared with just $9,000 for a housing subsidy that would keep the family together.

As evident in Exhibit 7.4, the net assets of WFCM are nonexistent compared to other comparable organizations. This is most likely the difference between owning a program facility and renting one. It was the dramatic increase in lease expenses for WFCM that has threatened the future of the organization.

The homeless in Fairfax County who are helped by WFCM come from all levels of society and all kinds of backgrounds. Consider Harry and his family who live in Chantilly, Virginia. Until he suffered a work-related back injury, Harry earned $70,000 per year, and his wife earned $20,000. They have two children in college and a mortgage on their house. After his back injury, Harry was terminated from employment, and, unable to find another job, found himself without health benefits, trying to live on his wife's income of $20,000. Finally, Harry swallowed his pride and turned to WFCM for assistance. They were able to help him avoid

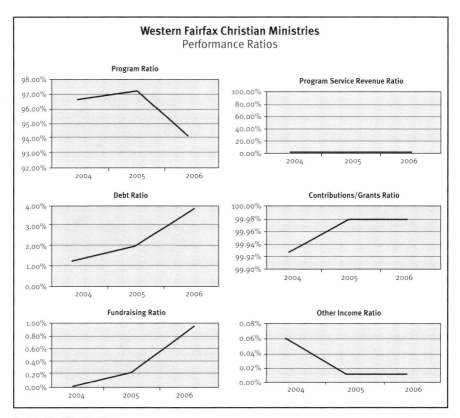

EXHIBIT 7.3   **WESTERN FAIRFAX CHRISTIAN MINISTRIES PERFORMANCE RATIOS**

SOURCE: GuideStar, www.guidestar.com.

foreclosure on the mortgage and provide a weekly supply of groceries to help him through his financial challenges. Harry and his family are not alone. In fact, there are over 2,000 homeless people in wealthy Fairfax County, where an individual must earn a minimum of $46,000 per year to have any chance of finding affordable housing. Of the homeless, 67% are under age 18, and 75% of the homeless families are headed by a single parent. Virtually all fall below the low-income levels established by HUD; 38% are black, 30% are white, 28% are Hispanic, and 4% are Asian.

Fairfax County Board of Supervisors chairman Gerald Connolly is an articulate advocate for the homeless, driving the county's vision to eliminate homelessness within ten years. "when you meet the homeless children,

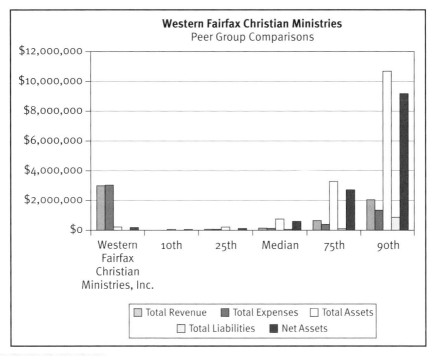

EXHIBIT 7.4   WESTERN FAIRFAX CHRISTIAN MINISTRIES PEER GROUP COMPARISONS

SOURCE: GuideStar, www.guidestar.com.

your heart breaks," said connolly.[3] speaking at the community summit to end homelessness in april 2007, connolly said, "homelessness is a problem across the united states; however in a region where the median household income is $88,133 annually and six fortune 500 companies sit in our backyard, we as a community actually have the resources to fix it. continuing to allow these members of our community to be homeless is simply unacceptable. the time has come to stop talking about managing homelessness and start planning to end it."

The president of the Federal Home Loan Mortgage Corporation (Freddie Mac), speaking at the Summit to End Homelessness, said, "[W]e are a proud citizen of Fairfax County. And when it comes to ending homelessness, we stand ready to act." Freddie Mac not only acts but writes checks, contributing over $700,000 per year in funding for social services programs focused on transitional housing.

Fairfax County has four strategies to eliminate homelessness in the county over the next 10 years:

1. Prevent homelessness due to economic crisis and disability
2. Preserve and increase affordable housing supply
3. Deliver services to obtain and maintain stable housing
4. Create a management system and ensure accountability

In August 2007, Fairfax County proudly opened the brand-new model 17,000-square-foot Katherine K. Hanley Family Shelter, offering temporary housing and support for up to 20 homeless families with children. Daily programming plugs children into public schools while parents work or search for work. Supplementing the school and work schedules is a complete array of social services support activities intended to help these families transition to financial independence. This is a significant addition to the county's three other shelters, with the potential to significantly reduce the backlog and waiting list for families in need of shelter. In addition to this model shelter, innovatively embedded in a new housing development, the county is also planning to build The Residences at the Government Center, a complex offering affordable housing to middle-income professionals such as schoolteachers and firefighters, with a mix of single-room-occupancy units for the homeless.

The U.S. Department of Housing and Urban Development (HUD) appropriates over $4 million per year to homeless assistance in Fairfax County. The county distributes over $10 million per year through the Community Funding Pool to support social services programs run by private entities including 20 faith-based organizations, such as Western Fairfax Christian Ministries, which is budgeted to receive a $190,000 appropriation for 2008. In recognition of the critical role that faith-based nonprofits play in the delivery of social services, the county maintains the Community Interfaith Office for the purpose of strengthening communications and facilitating collaborative efforts between the county government and the faith-based social services providers.

But faith-based organizations, even those serving people in great need, get no pass on the need for financial prudence. Faith and prudence are not mutually exclusive. There is no inherent need for conflict between the county's need for financial accountability and the rights of a faith-based organization. In fact, the doctrinal origins of faith-based organizations and teachings of stewardship should cause these organizations to lead the parade on both financial accountability and prudence in financial management.

This tale is primarily about the need for financial accountability and prudent management. Rapid expansion of program and overhead expenses, coupled with the failure of the board to demand fiscal prudence and accountability of management in the shadow of jubilant growth and passion for ministry, led WFCM into the Zone of Insolvency, with more than half of the staff losing jobs. This in a county that recognizes the need to fund programs that will reduce and eliminate homelessness. If WFCM ultimately closes its doors, it will not be due to the lack of county funding, nor will it be for lack of need for their services. Fiscal management may not be the reason many mission-driven staff show up for work, but the mission will ultimately fail without sustainable funding and fiscal responsibility.

Key Lessons

Rapid Growth Can Lead to Financial Distress

Rapid growth, including significant increases in revenue, can be difficult to manage. Reading a financial statement that is relatively static year after year is totally different from assessing rapid changes in financial statements. Sometimes significant increases in funding mask even greater increases in expense commitments resulting from lag time on payments due. Furthermore, predicting the sustainability of rapid growth is tricky business; will the growth continue at the same rate, flatten out, peak, or drop?

The Underfunded, Overworked Trap

Demand for an organization's services does not guarantee success. In the case of Fairfax County and WFCM, there is clearly demand for services. The real issue is not the demand but the sustainability of adequate funding. There is no shortage of government contracts that partially fund programs or services, transferring to private charities the need to raise additional funds to subsidize delivery of services. But these arrangements can quickly leave the charity overcommitted and underfunded.

Fixed Overhead Can Create Jeopardy

Failure to understand the difference between direct and indirect expenses along with the implications of expense trends can place an organization in peril. It is common for nonprofit executives to have minimal training or understanding of the implications of fixed expenses. In the case of WFCM, the 2003 excitement about relocating to a larger facility was subsequently tempered by the harsh realities of the noncancellable five-year lease that cost 900% over the previous lease annually and created a $400,000 tail-end obligation. If the revenue had continued to increase at the same rate, the lease would not have been a problem. But immediately after signing the new lease, the organization was faced with decreasing revenue, and the combination was devastating.

FIVE GREAT QUESTIONS FOR YOUR NEXT BOARD MEETING

1. Does this organization have a sustainable fundraising model?
2. How is the environment changing, and how will that impact the financial demands on our organization?
3. Is it possible that meeting an increasing demand will actually push this organization into financial distress?
4. Do we clearly understand trends in our fixed overheads?
5. Are we investing appropriately to build a sustainable fundraising system?

NOTES

1. Jacqueline, Salmon, "A Charity Finds Itself in Dire Need," *Fairfax Extra*, July 26, 2007, pp. 16–17.
2. William, Flook, "Nonprofit's Closing Forestalled While It Seeks Financial Solutions," *The Examiner*, May 8, 2007.
3. Wendy, Koch, "Homelessness Catches Families Even Amid Affluence," *USA Today*, December 22, 2006.

CHAPTER 8

American Red Cross

AGGRESSIVE STANCE AGAINST FRAUD

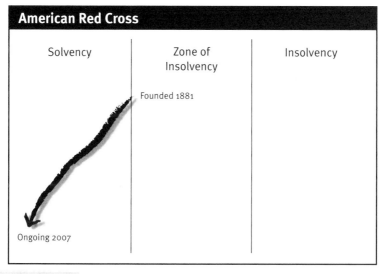

American Red Cross

Solvency	Zone of Insolvency	Insolvency
	Founded 1881	
Ongoing 2007		

EXHIBIT 8.1   AMERICAN RED CROSS FINANCIAL PATH

In May 2007, a retired accountant for the Orange County, California, chapter of the American Red Cross pleaded guilty to charges of embezzling more than $100,000. She used the organization's traveler's checks and credit card on shopping sprees, to pay expenses at Sam's Town Hotel and Gambling Hall in Las Vegas,[1] to make purchases at Home Depot, to pay for an underwater camera, jewelry, a vacation at the Hilton Hawaiian Village, Major League Baseball tickets, and a membership in the

San Diego Zoo. Her accounting duties over 17 years involved ordering traveler's checks for workers embarking on disaster-relief missions. The theft was discovered upon her retirement when her replacement could not make the books balance and called for an investigation, which was subsequently handed over to the FBI. The thief will face up to two years in prison and will be required to pay restitution (see Exhibit 8.1).[2]

"The American Red Cross has a very aggressive stance against fraud and works closely with law enforcement when criminal activity is discovered," said Stanley V. Purdue, chief executive officer. "The American Red Cross has a zero tolerance policy toward fraud. We are grateful for the diligent work of the FBI and the Assistant U.S. Attorney in bringing this matter to justice." The Assistant U.S. Attorney prosecuting the case indicated that the Red Cross noticed discrepancies and called for the audit in 2006.[3]

The American Red Cross, founded by Clara Barton in 1881, currently has 35,000 employees operating in 800 chapters, generating $3.8 billion per year. The Orange County, California, chapter, founded in 1965, features 60 employees and annual revenue of $6 million. In service to Orange County's three million residents in 2006, the Orange County Red Cross responded to 148 incidents, assisted 230 families impacted by disasters, and provided 4,500 meals, beverages, and snacks for disaster victims and emergency responders (see Exhibit 8.2).

In May 2007, the board of the American Red Cross (National Headquarters) announced the appointment of the former head of the Internal Revenue Service, Mark Everson, as the third Red Cross chief executive in the past eight years. "People said it's a tough position, but running the Internal Revenue Service was a grown-up job," said Everson. "I like a challenge, and I think I can help the organization." Both organizations have tens of thousands of employees, and both report to Congress. When. Everson took over, the American Red Cross had an operating deficit in spite of unprecedented giving in 2006, with gifts designated primarily to the Katrina fund and not available for general operating purposes. To trim expenses, he may need to announce staffing cuts in the national headquarters, which currently employs 3,000.[4]

The saga of the Orange County chapter accountant is significant in principle and instructive in regard to the aggressive response of the Red Cross. With 35,000 employees, it may be impossible to prevent every

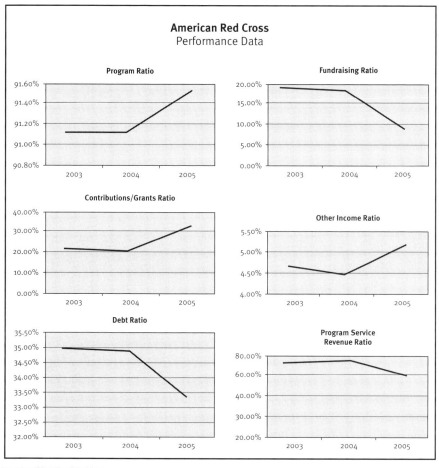

EXHIBIT 8.2   AMERICAN RED CROSS PERFORMANCE DATA

SOURCE: GuideStar, www.guidestar.com.

possibility of criminal activity, but the Red Cross stands ready to respond to any indication of such a problem and will leave no stone unturned in its quests for justice to protect the donors' dollars.

The breaking news at the American Red Cross in August 2007 was another story about fiduciary responsibility—the lawsuit by Johnson & Johnson filed against the Red Cross in August 2007 for use of the Red Cross symbol. For more than 100 years, the American Red Cross and pharmaceutical giant Johnson & Johnson have shared the red cross symbol.

The American Red Cross used the symbol as an icon for disaster relief, whereas Johnson & Johnson used the symbol on commercial products. But in 2004, the American Red Cross followed the path of Habitat for Humanity and the American Heart Association and began licensing use of its icon to for-profit companies selling a variety of health and medical products.[5]

Red Cross CEO Mark Everson described Johnson & Johnson's suit as "obscene . . . so that J&J can make more money."

"What we're talking about here is their deviation from a long-standing partnership and collaboration around the use of this trademark and their push to commercialize this trademark in the for-profit arena," said Jeffrey J. Leebaw, a spokesman for Johnson & Johnson. "We deeply regret that it has become necessary to file this complaint. The company has the highest regard for the American Red Cross and its mission."[6] It is not surprising that the American Red Cross is moving in the direction of licensed sponsorships that generate income in return for approved use of the icon. In fact, given the tremendous power of the icon, it could be irresponsible not to utilize the asset to drive additional income for the charity.

Giant nonprofit organizations now recognize their high-value brand potential for significant income based on corporate sponsorships from companies anxious to be identified with the positive aspects of these brands. Habitat for Humanity recently had its brand independently appraised and valued at $1.8 billion. Based on that valuation, Habitat doubled its sponsorship income from $16 million in 2002 to $40 million in 2004. The United Way brand was recently appraised at $34.7 billion, ranking it just behind Coca-Cola, Microsoft, IBM, and GE and just ahead of Intel and Disney.[7] Clearly, protecting a brand asset appraised in the billions of dollars is an evolving area of fiduciary responsibility foreign to most nonprofit boards.

In summary, the Orange County Red Cross theft is an elegantly simple tale of greed and temptation played out over a 17-year career. In return for her poor choices, the accountant gets two years of free room and board in a prison cell and will spend the rest of her life paying restitution. The image of the Red Cross was protected, if not enhanced, by decisive action that demonstrates its commitment to integrity and accountability for all employees. The Red Cross positioned itself well by calling for the audit, inviting in the state attorney general, and cooperating with the FBI, while touting its zero-tolerance policy in regard to criminal activity. Financial losses were minimized and will be recouped, leaving the organization in a position of fiscal strength. Charity Navigator gives the American Red Cross a resounding rating, indicating that 91.5% of funds are spent on program expenses, just 4.9% on administrative expenses, and only 3.4% on fundraising expenses. At the local and international level, dealing with relatively small dollar amounts or potentially hundreds of millions, the Red Cross is committed to integrity and must continue to generate income from donations and other innovative means, such as licensed sponsorships, in order to continue in its never-ending mission of providing disaster relief.

KEY LESSONS

Size Is an Advantage in Dealing with Wrongdoers

Larger organizations have more resources to bring to bear in investigating wrongdoers and establishing systems to reduce the possibility for wrongdoing. The same systems are disproportionately expensive for smaller organizations. This does not excuse board or management of smaller organizations from their fiduciary responsibilities. Given the size of the American Red Cross, the number of dollars managed annually, and the number of employees, it has a remarkably low incidence of criminal behavior.

Size Is a Larger Target for Wrongdoers

Size may have advantages, but the sheer scope of the American Red Cross and the dollars it manages make it a prime target for scam artists and wrongdoers. In fact, recent news reports have focused on scam artists claiming to represent the American Red Cross who are calling families of deployed military personnel and illicitly gathering confidential information. Regardless of the size of the organization, every effort must be taken to prevent wrongdoers from taking advantage of it.

Evolving Fiduciary Responsibilities

The board of the American Red Cross understands its role and acts quickly and aggressively in regard to fraud or embezzlement. At the same time, the board is growing in its understanding of what it means to protect a brand asset appraised in the billions of dollars.

FIVE GREAT QUESTIONS FOR YOUR NEXT BOARD MEETING

1. Do we have a zero-tolerance policy in regard to criminal activity as well as a plan to act accordingly?
2. Have we considered the value of our brand, and are we managing that asset appropriately?
3. Would we pursue justice in the event of a crime, or would we prefer to settle quietly in hopes of avoiding publicity?
4. What policies do we have in place to protect and enhance the asset value of our brand?
5. Do we have adequate whistleblower protections in place?

NOTES

1. Mai, Tran, "Ex-Red Cross Accountant Indicted; The Woman, Who Worked for the O.C. Chapter Is Accused of Taking $100,000 for Personal Use," *Los Angeles Times,* January 18, 2007, section B, p. 1.
2. David, Haldane, "Plea Deal Is Set in Thefts from O.C. Red Cross," *Los Angeles Times,* May 23, 2007, section B, p. 10.
3. Randal, Archibald, "Ex-Official of Red Cross Is Charged with Fraud," *New York Times,* January 18, 2007, section A, p. 14.
4. Ian, Wilhelm, "New Red Cross Leader Announces His Priorities," *The Chronicle of Philanthropy,* June 28, 2007.
5. Stephanie, Saul, "Johnson & Johnson Sues Red Cross Over Symbol," *New York Times,* August 9, 2007.
6. Ibid.
7. Holly, Hall, "What's in a Charity's Name?" *The Chronicle of Philanthropy,* August 5, 2004.

CHAPTER 9

Electronic Industries Alliance

DISSOLUTION CELEBRATION

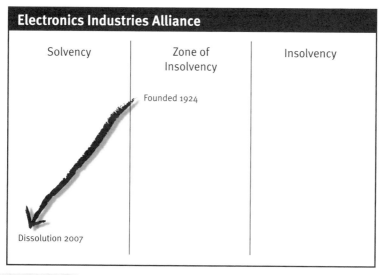

Electronics Industries Alliance

| Solvency | Zone of Insolvency | Insolvency |

Founded 1924

Dissolution 2007

EXHIBIT 9.1   **ELECTRONIC INDUSTRIES ALLIANCE FINANCIAL PATH**

In July 2007, the board of the Electronic Industries Alliance (EIA), 1924–2007, voted for dissolution and will distribute over $36 million in net assets between the four remaining member associations. These include the Electronics Components Assemblies & Materials Association (ECA), the Internet Security Alliance, the Telecommunications Industry Association (TIA), and the Government Electronics and Information Technology Association (GEIA), along with the founding member of the alliance, the Consumer Electronics Association. The action was based on the belief that realignment of its member associations had rendered the EIA powerless, "a virtual puppet." "We believe these changes will dramatically enhance the ability of these four groups to meet their objectives, be they improved advocacy in Washington or enhanced services for member companies," said Mike Kennedy, EIA chair and Motorola senior vice president.[1] Founded as the Radio Manufacturers Association, the Electronic Industries Association is the premier advocate for the $400 billion electronics industry, representing more than 1,300 member companies through its four primary associations (see Exhibit 9.1).

As shown in Exhibit 9.2, EIA carries a very positive fund balance in spite of a decrease in 2005. Exhibit 9.3 shows a variance in net gains annually for the period 2001 to 2005. This appears to be a controlled net, with strategic control of expenses to minimize excess build up of cash reserves. Exhibit 9.4 appears to demonstrate that management is working

EXHIBIT 9.2 **ELECTRONIC INDUSTRIES ALLIANCE BALANCE SHEET**

Electronic Industries Alliance			
Balance Sheet: Fiscal Year Ending December 31, 2005			
ASSETS	**January 1, 2005**	**December 31, 2005**	**Change**
Cash & Equivalent	$4,875,000	$3,210,251	($1,664,845)
Accounts Receivable	$917,053	$1,214,490	$297,437
Pledges & Grants Receivable	$1,500,000	$0	($1,500,000)
Receivable/Other	$433,741	$2,333,741	$1,900,000
Inventories for Sale of Use	$0	$0	$0
Investment/Securities	$19,557,055	$18,771,011	($786,044)
Investment/Other	$0	$0	$0
Fixed Assets	$11,592,785	$11,159,749	($433,036)
Other	$51,967	$11,506	($40,461)
Total Assets	**$38,927,697**	**$36,700,748**	**($2,226,949)**
LIABILITIES			
Accounts Payable	$2,225,743	$1,253,510	($972,233)
Grants Payable	$0	$0	$0
Deferred Revenue	$418,576	$668,300	$249,724
Loans and Notes	$0	$0	$0
Tax-Exempt Bond Liabilities	$0	$0	$0
Other	$1,952,066	$1,788,561	($163,505)
Total Liabilities	$4,596,385	$3,710,371	($886,014)
Fund Balance	**$34,331,312**	**$32,990,377**	**($1,340,935)**

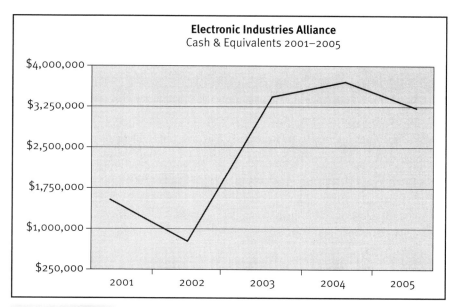

EXHIBIT 9.3   **ELECTRONIC INDUSTRIES ALLIANCE CASH & EQUIVALENTS**

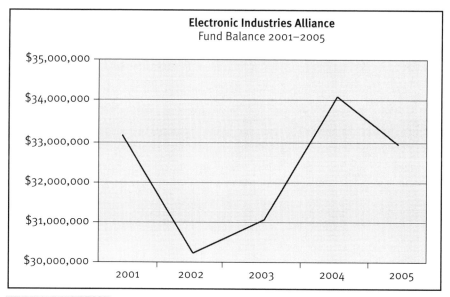

EXHIBIT 9.4   **ELECTRONIC INDUSTRIES ALLIANCE FUND BALANCE**

strategically with budget to maintain net assets level between $31 million and $33 million.

David McCurdy served as CEO of EIA from October 1998 to December 2006, when he resigned to move to a new position as CEO of the Alliance of Automobile Manufacturers. During his previous 14 years in the House of Representatives, Representative McCurdy served as chair of the House Intelligence Committee, chair of the Military Installations and Facilities Subcommittee of the House Armed Services Committee, and chair of the Transportation Aviation and Materials Subcommittee of the Science and Space Committee. He was cofounder and chair of the Democratic Leadership Council. McCurdy is highly regarded as a lobbyist and association executive.

> Charles Darwin observed that it is not the strongest nor the most intelligent that survive, but the ones most responsive to change. The September 11 attacks were brilliantly evil; they were entirely "outside the box" of what we thought likely. Now it is our turn to adapt. To win this new war, government must change how it thinks and acts and do a much better job of coordinating its assets.

These were McCurdy's closing remarks in testimony before the Senate Committee on Government Affairs regarding a bill to establish the National Commission on Terrorist Attacks Upon the United States, February 2002. His poignant summary of Darwin could just as readily have been applied to leadership in the nonprofit sector. The ability to adapt and think outside the box is critical to long-term success in an ever-changing environment.

"Change is the only constant in today's high-tech business," said Mike Kennedy, EIA's chairman of the board and Motorola senior vice president.

"The resultant new structure will allow each sector to have a stronger focus on its core interest area, while maintaining cross-industry connections," said Jim Shiring, Microsemi Corporation executive vice president, who also serves as EIA's secretary/treasurer.

"ECA supports this new structure, which will expand our ability to deliver innovative international conferences and symposiums," said James R. Kaplan, Sr., ECA's chairman of the board and Cornell Dubilier Electronics chair and CEO. "These changes will also enhances ECA's standing as a leader in the development and implementation of international standards.

"These changes will provide our members with the ability under GEIA auspices to address public policy issues on Capitol Hill and throughout the executive agencies," said Dan Heinemeier, president of GEIA. "We are excited at the prospect of building on the strong heritage of the EIA government relations program."

"TIA strongly supports this realignment, which improves the value proposition for TIA members, strengthens the voice of TIA's advocacy and creates new opportunities for all parties," said Rob Pullen, TIA's chair of the board and Tellabs senior vice president.

This is an important tale about an organization that managed to avoid the Zone of Insolvency, built significant assets in the process of serving its members, yet was proactive in dissolution, even though it has significant net assets, positive cash flow, and 83 years of service to members. It is a story of a board and membership with the integrity and transparency to admit that in spite of a strong financial position, they were no longer making a unique contribution. Rather than sustain the organization just because they could, they voted to celebrate success and close it down, redistributing the assets to nonprofit organizations better prepared to serve in the future, thereby strengthening the nonprofit community at large.

Key Lessons

Power Does Not Dictate Continuance

EIA benefited in recent years from the leadership of CEO David McCurdy, arguably one of the most powerful association executives in the country. Under his leadership, the association continued to exert great influence on public policy, delivering real benefits to a $400 billion industry. But power does not necessitate continuance. When the environment changes, it is time to think outside of the box, and sometimes that requires applying radical change to corporate structures.

Cash Reserves Do Not Dictate Continuance

Positive cash flow and significant cash reserves may make an organization an unsinkable ship, but they do not dictate the need for continuance. Too many managers and board members perpetuate nonprofit organizations because they can—that is, because the cash position enables continuance.

The result can be an organization in search of a mission. Bold is the board that declares a mission complete, even with cash reserves on hand.

History of Success Does Not Demand Continuance

There is no doubt about the significant history of success of the Electronic Industries Alliance. But choosing to dissolve does not necessarily dishonor history. The two are not mutually exclusive. There is no requirement that a nonprofit stay in business just to honor its history. If the mission is complete or the business model is no longer sustainable, it's time to celebrate the successes and move on.

FIVE GREAT QUESTIONS FOR YOUR NEXT BOARD MEETING

1. Do we continue our enterprise simply because it is financially viable, or because it still has a functional capacity to achieve its mission?
2. If this organization was not likely to achieve its mission moving forward, would we as a board have the courage to file for dissolution?
3. Do our assets generate enough social return on investment to justify our continuance, or would it be more responsible to file for dissolution and distribute the assets to other nonprofits better positioned to carry the mission forward?
4. In the event of dissolution, what would be our net asset remaining after all wind-down expenses?
5. To which organizations would we consider distributing any remaining assets in the event of dissolution?

▦ NOTES

1. Tavia, Gilchrist, "EIA's Board Votes to Dissolve Trade Group," *CEO Update,* vol. 17, no. 430 (2007), p. 6.

CHAPTER 10

Women in Community Service

"KNOW WHEN TO FOLD 'EM"

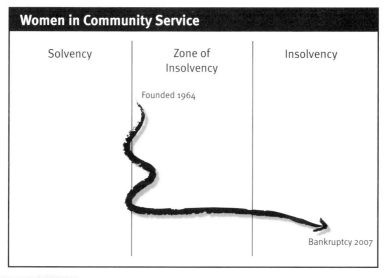

Women in Community Service

Solvency	Zone of Insolvency	Insolvency

Founded 1964

Bankruptcy 2007

EXHIBIT 10.1   **WOMEN IN COMMUNITY SERVICE FINANCIAL PATH**

In August 2007, Women in Community Service (WICS) ceased operations and filed for bankruptcy, ending 43 years of service (see Exhibit 10.1). (In the interest of total disclosure, the reader should know that the author managed the organization through a consulting contract as interim chief executive officer during its final five months.)

Like the National Alliance of Business, WICS rose out of the poverty programs of the 1960s, inspired by John F. Kennedy and focused on life skills training for women in transition. Dependent on government funding since the early years, WICS found that government contracts were shifting more and more risk onto the organization while increasing the demand for fundraising to offset budget limitations. But raising charitable contributions to supplement services delivered by government contracts proved increasingly difficult.

Over the years WICS served more than 2 million women and young people living in poverty by promoting self-reliance and economic independence, providing the training, resources, and inspiration necessary to transition from poverty to self sufficiency. In recent years, programming also included life skills training for women and young people in transition from welfare to work, incarceration to community living, public housing to ownership, and homelessness to employment and independence. As a Job Corps contractor, WICS most recently took the lead role in piloting the signature program of the Director of the Department of Labor, offering a new approach to inspirational leadership and mentoring.

The WICS board began to consider the possibility of closure several years ago. Deficits were increasing, as shown in Exhibit 10.1, and cash reserves were dwindling, as shown in Exhibit 10.2. Government contracts were moving to performance-based payments that put the organization at greater financial risk, fundraising was increasingly challenging, and the core mission of the organization was becoming difficult to identify. Some board members felt that it was time to cease operations and celebrate the successes, while other board members and management felt compelled to keep the organization alive in order to honor its history. A closedown analysis in 2005 focused the debate, but the board chose to continue to try every means possible to keep the organization operational and turn it around to fiscal strength. Then, in 2007, a government contract providing a major share of revenue was significantly reduced, and the board decided to cease operations.

In announcing the closure, WICS board chair Mary Ann Wyrsch noted WICS's strong record of accomplishment over the past four decades in guiding women and young people facing poverty toward lives of financial and personal independence. "Many individuals—including WICS' program participants, volunteers, staff, and supporters—are a part of WICS' success and history," she said. "We want to celebrate that legacy."

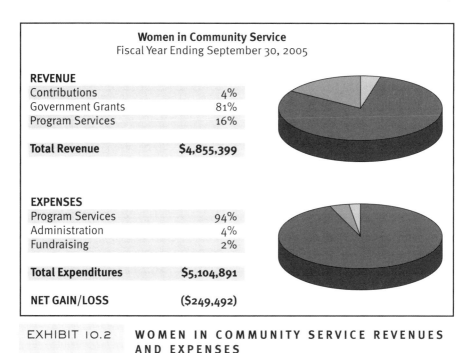

Women in Community Service
Fiscal Year Ending September 30, 2005

REVENUE
Contributions	4%
Government Grants	81%
Program Services	16%

Total Revenue   **$4,855,399**

EXPENSES
Program Services	94%
Administration	4%
Fundraising	2%

Total Expenditures   **$5,104,891**

NET GAIN/LOSS   **($249,492)**

EXHIBIT 10.2   **WOMEN IN COMMUNITY SERVICE REVENUES AND EXPENSES**

SOURCE: GuideStar, www.guidestar.com.

A former WICS client in Portland, Oregon, spoke of her gratitude to WICS. "I had been in and out of prison eight times until I found WICS," she said. "WICS Lifeskills gave me the survival skills that I was lacking, the ones that I needed to keep me out of prison. I owe my new life to WICS. Today I am a housing specialist/case manager for the Recuperation Care Program of Central City Concern. Here, I work with individuals who are struggling in all the areas that I struggled to overcome. WICS prepared me for this job. I am certain that without the training and confidence I received I would not be who I am today. Because I was helped, I now help others."

"I was proud to be a part of WICS from its very beginning," said Dr. Dorothy I. Height, chair and president emerita of the National Council of Negro Women. "From its earliest days, WICS has had thousands of volunteers—black, white, brown, Protestant, Catholic, Jewish, poor, middle class, and affluent—who worked together serving and supporting young people who wanted to help themselves out of poverty. WICS has been an American treasure. Its legacy will be the hundreds of thousands

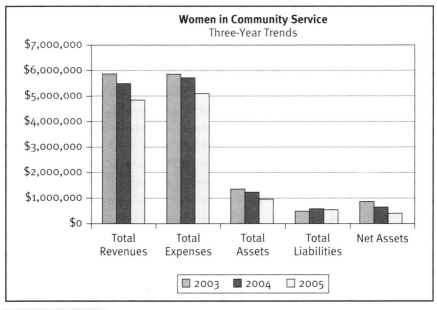

EXHIBIT 10.3   **WOMEN IN COMMUNITY SERVICE THREE-YEAR TRENDS**

SOURCE: GuideStar, www.guidestar.com.

of lives that have been touched and doors that have been opened as a result of its work," Dr. Height stated.

The WICS performance ratios in Exhibit 10.3 are particularly enlightening, given the subsequent filing for bankruptcy.

The program ratio dropped from 2003 to 2005, indicating that the organization was actually spending a decreasing percentage of its gross revenue on charitable activities. This is typical of an organization in transition, which finds itself spending more on managing its affairs and transitions.

The debt ratio increased from 40% to 60% in three years. This ratio is based on a formula that compares total liabilities against total assets. In the case of WICS, there was no real debt, but the assets were being depleted rapidly, causing the precipitous rise in this ratio.

The fundraising ratio rose and fell in three years, driven by a fundraising vacancy, subsequent hiring, and second vacancy.

The contributions/grants ratio shows a decrease in funding from government service contracts, and grants. With income from grants being less than the expense of servicing these contracts, WICS was in effect subsidizing services rendered out of cash reserves.

The other income ratio indicates a minor three-year fluctuation, but consistent with the experience of most charities, this category of income totaled less than 10%.

Finally, in Exhibit 10.4 we see a revealing comparison with peer organizations. First, WICS recorded expenses in excess of revenues, the reverse of peer organizations that recorded net gains, not deficits. Second, we see that WICS had total assets equal to approximately one-fifth of gross revenue, compared with peer organizations that showed total assets equal to approximately three-quarters of gross revenue. Third, total liabilities at WICS were equal to approximately 60% of total assets, but for peer organizations

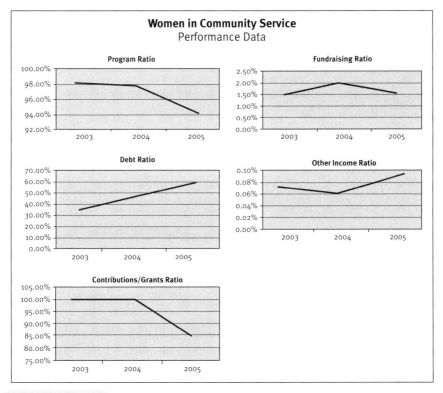

EXHIBIT 10.4   **WOMEN IN COMMUNITY SERVICE PERFORMANCE DATA**

SOURCE: GuideStar, www.guidestar.com.

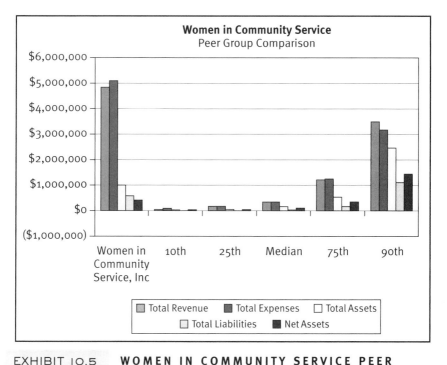

EXHIBIT 10.5   **WOMEN IN COMMUNITY SERVICE PEER GROUP COMPARISON**

SOURCE: GuideStar, www.guidestar.com.

liabilities were approximately 35% of assets (see Exhibit 10.5). Finally, the net assets as a percentage of gross expense amounted to less than 10% for WICS, but more than 35% for peer organizations.

This is the tale of an organization that served well, fought hard to reposition itself in a changing environment, and found it difficult to contemplate dissolution. Every effort was made by board and management to transition the organization to more sustainable contracts with more cost-efficient operations. The dissolution debate resurfaced over a period of years, with reserves dwindling, while management tried new contracts and new fundraising activities to turn the organization around. Finally, with a major reduction in a large contract, the board concluded that the organization was simply no longer fiscally viable. Making every last effort to keep the mission alive in order to honor history, WICS ultimately responded to funding cuts by filing for bankruptcy.

The bankruptcy filing, a public document, indicates that the organization was current on payables at the time of filing and carried no debt.

Unfortunately, with reduced government contract revenue, WICS was not viable moving forward and unable to meet the tail-end obligations on several office leases. During the past few years, board and management had succeeded in reducing tail-end obligations on leases, but the obligations were still too high at the time of the contract reductions. As a standard accounting practice, tail-end lease obligations are not listed as liabilities on the balance sheet until a corporation closes. At that point, the complete lease payments for all remaining months due under the terms of the list are added to the balance sheet. If, for example, an organization owes $10,000 a month rent and has 12 months remaining on the lease, a total liability of $120,000 would be recorded on the balance sheet.

When a board contemplates closing a nonprofit organization, it must carefully consider the interests of all parties of the corporations, including members, customers, donors, stakeholders, clients, patients, students, creditors, and staff. These deliberations are often complicated, given that some of these parties, at times, may seem to be in conflict with each other. For example, while employees typically want to remain employed, this must be weighed against the interests of the creditors or even the donors. Inevitably, some board members will argue that the duty of the board is to keep the organization alive at all costs, while others will believe that continuing is irresponsible.

Key Lessons

Board Considerations of Dissolution Are Complicated

The courts have determined that a board governing an organization in the Zone of Insolvency (including those in the process of closing) has expanded legal responsibilities, requiring that it balance the interests of all parties of the corporation. This moves the board from focused fiduciary responsibility for the assets of the corporation to a consideration of the interests of donors, creditors, staff, patients, clients, customers, and the community at large.

Tail-End Obligations Add to the Expense of Closure

Take a good look at your organization's balance sheet. It will change in the process of dissolution, with tail-end obligations added to the total liabilities. Add to that expenses for attorneys and close-out consultants.

Subtract some portion of receivables from the assets listed on the balance sheet in anticipation of slow pay once word of the dissolution is made public.

Closing an Organization Does Not Necessarily Dishonor Its History

It is quite possible that a nonprofit corporation can have a history of high-impact success and yet find itself in a changed environment where its job is finished or the organization is no longer financially viable. The decision to close is not a decision to dishonor that history. WICS is an excellent example of an organization that served well and can rightfully celebrate its legacy even as it recognizes the financial realities and closes. There is no legal or ethical requirement that board members keep an organization alive at all costs. If, in the judgment of the board, the interests of all parties of the organization are not best served by continuance, then the vote for dissolution is appropriate and necessary.

FIVE GREAT QUESTIONS FOR YOUR NEXT BOARD MEETING

1. Does this board understand the total costs of closing?
2. Are we as a board aware of our legal duty to protect the interests of all parties of the corporation in the Zone of Insolvency or during closure considerations?
3. What do our performance metrics reveal about the condition of this organization?
4. What compelling reason do we have to remain in operation?
5. What rationale do we have for merger or dissolution?

PART TWO

Naming the Disease

Perhaps you may remember the early discussions around the disease that we now commonly refer to as AIDS. In the late 1970s and early 1980s, reference to the disease was awkward. There were stories of symptoms, and descriptions, but there was no simple name that was recognized by the public at large. Researchers had observations, but it was difficult to define the disease and therefore difficult to solicit funding for research. Newsmagazines referred to this mysterious thing called Acquired Immune Deficiency Syndrome, but it was hard to remember and hardly seemed like a name for a disease. Over time, the public began to understand references to AIDS. The name stuck, and work began in earnest on fundraising for research to develop cures.

There is a syndrome, or disease, impacting several hundred thousand nonprofit organizations. It has a name: the Zone of Insolvency—a name most board members and managers have never heard. If your organization is living in financial distress, you need to name the disease, understand the symptoms, identify the risks, and work on a cure.

CHAPTER 11

Detecting the Zone of Insolvency

Definitions would be good things if we did not use words to make them.

—JEAN-JACQUES ROUSSEAU

Detecting the Zone of Insolvency would be easy if there were flashing red lights and sirens to alert the board and management that an organization had crossed into the zone. Boards might not realize that they are operating in the zone until after the fact, when their earlier decisions are second-guessed by the courts. In fact, many board members have never heard of the Zone of Insolvency. The closest thing to flashing red lights and sirens for nonprofits entering the zone is a "going concerns" finding in an annual audit, but this is often too little too late.

The Zone of Insolvency has been defined as a period of financial distress during which prudent people could at least foresee the possibility of insolvency (see Exhibit 11.1). This is particularly problematic for non-profit organizations because such a high percentage of nonprofits live perpetually in financial distress. Acting out of a passion for the mission and a desire to serve, nonprofit leaders have a tendency to tolerate financial distress that would rarely be accepted in the for-profit arena.

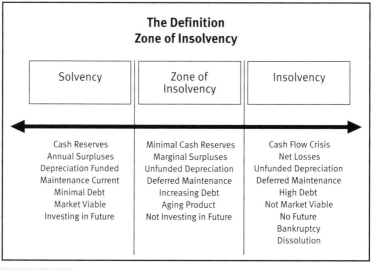

EXHIBIT 11.1   ZONE OF INSOLVENCY DEFINED

THE BALANCE SHEET TEST FOR SOLVENCY

The most common test for solvency focuses on the balance of assets versus liabilities. If the liabilities exceed the assets, there is an assumption of insolvency. If the assets exceed liabilities, there is an assumption of insolvency. While this test serves a purpose, it is not always accurate. For example, a new and fast-growing corporation might have high profits and great cash flow, but in the process of acquiring buildings or equipment, it might also carry very high levels of debt. In this case, the liabilities exceed the assets, but the company is healthy and able to service the debt level through cash flow.

THE CASH FLOW TEST FOR SOLVENCY

This leads to the second test for solvency, the cash flow test. Corporations in an expansion stage of development are often forced to borrow in order to build facilities and acquire equipment. Provided that the cash flow is sufficient and sustainable and the debt level is within reasonable ratios, these corporations must be considered solvent even if liabilities exceed assets. While one might argue strategically for a long-term position with assets in excess of liabilities, the short-term strategy of servicing debt from cash flow cannot be disallowed. In the discussion of AHERF in Chapter 1, we saw how the inability to handle the cash flow, ultimately resulting in the loss of millions per month, led to bankruptcy.

The Dissolution Test for Solvency

A third test for solvency considers the ability to file for dissolution and pay off all creditors at 100%. In this regard, both the balance sheet test and the cash flow tests fall short of telling the complete story. Consider, for instance, a corporation with minimal assets but enough cash flow to stay current on payables and on contractual obligations with long tail ends, such as executive contracts or a five-year lease for office space. The lease payments are budgeted and paid on time, and, in keeping with generally accepted accounting principles, the tail-end obligation of the lease is not identified on the balance sheet as a liability. Using the balance sheet test and the cash flow test, this corporation would appear to be solvent as long as it continues to operate. But if it were to close down, the tail-end obligations on the lease would immediately be added to the balance sheet. Suddenly there would be no cash flow, and the liabilities would far exceed the assets. In other words, if the organization were to file for dissolution, it could not pay all of its obligations and would need to seek the protection of the bankruptcy courts to distribute the remaining assets as equitably as possible to the creditors.

Fixed Overhead Ratios

Overhead factors vary greatly from organization to organization and from sector to sector. For example, universities and hospitals have huge investments in physical plant and therefore high fixed overhead. These facilities represent fixed expense that does not vary significantly with volume. If the number of students or patients decreases, the same fixed overhead must be spread over fewer paying customers, making it disproportionately more expensive. Increasing the customer base decreases the fixed overhead cost per customer. The higher the fixed overhead ratio, the more vulnerable the bottom line is to fluctuations in volume. Prudent managers and boards will pay special attention to fixed overhead factors to minimize volume-sensitive risk.

Net Gains

As nonprofit organizations move to performance-based funding and performance-based compensation, the choice of performance measures too often focuses on gross revenue rather than net gains. Perhaps this is consistent with the focus on mission, and the gross is somehow viewed as a measure of the volume of mission work achieved; the greater the gross, the greater the level of mission work achieved. Perhaps it flows from some deep-seated belief that profit or net is not appropriate for a nonprofit organization.

When the board or management sets performance expectations that drive gross revenue rather than net gain, the result usually drives the organization deeper into the Zone of Insolvency. Whereas for-profit corporations are expected to generate margin for research and development, new product development, and profit, nonprofits often forgo all of these and settle for "break even." But without net gain to build reserves, there is no capital to invest in new product or program development. The organization that does not invest in the future will ultimately fall behind the market, lose relevance, and find itself less than viable.

Net Assets

The level of net assets can be a significant factor in evaluating fiscal viability. With higher net worth, an organization may have greater ability to sustain losses and manage cash flow fluctuations through borrowing. With minimal net worth, ability to borrow to manage cash flow fluctuations is severely limited. Because receivables are listed as assets on the balance sheet, special care must be taken to evaluate the likelihood of ever collecting those receivables. One of the lessons from the case of Baptist Foundation of Arizona, presented in Chapter 6, was that the overstated receivables painted the picture of solvency when the organization was in fact insolvent.

Liquidity

Depending on the type of assets, an organization may have high or low liquidity. If the net asset is all cash, the organization has maximum liquidity and therefore the ability to move quickly without waiting periods or penalties for selling assets. But if all assets are tied up in real estate during a market downturn, or tied up in securities investments with heavy penalties for early liquidation, it may be asset rich with minimal ability to respond to opportunities or cash fluctuations.

UNFUNDED LIABILITIES

Two areas of unfunded liabilities are common problems for nonprofit organizations: (1) the problem of unfunded depreciation and (2) the problem of unfunded liabilities for donor restricted charitable gifts.

Recently the management and board of Alliance Redwoods closed the church retreat and conference facility for the first time in 60 years and borrowed $2 million to overhaul sewer, water, and electrical infrastructure. The infrastructure was failing following decades of deferred maintenance. Since the organization did not book or fund depreciation, the liability of the failing systems did not appear on the balance sheet until it was forced to borrow the $2 million. The decision to borrow was a business decision designed to avoid further business interruption due to infrastructure failures, but servicing the debt will challenge leadership for years to come.

No moral, legal, or ethical issue is involved here, but deferred maintenance and depreciation have consequences as undeniable as the laws of gravity. Nonprofit organizations have three options in regard to depreciation: (1) choose not to book depreciation, (2) choose to book depreciation but not fund it, or (3) choose to book depreciation and fund it. By choosing not to book or fund depreciation and further exacerbating the problem by budgeting too little for maintenance and deferred maintenance, Alliance Redwoods had a distorted picture of its true financial situation. That picture was considerably more focused by the addition of a $2 million loan to the balance sheet.

This tale has not yet ended. It is a harsh reality that depreciation and maintenance can be deferred, but they will ultimately demand payment. The proactive board and management team will position themselves ahead of this issue by realistic budgeting, including booking and funding depreciation and maintenance. The reactive board avoids these issues only to find that depreciation and deferred maintenance take their toll and demand attention at the most inconvenient of times. The Alliance Redwoods board and management team have identified the problem and are resolute in their desire to move from the Zone of Insolvency to long-term fiscal strength. The challenge now is to pay for the depreciation and deferred maintenance of the past 60 years (i.e., the loan) and at the same time pay forward by adequate funding of maintenance and depreciation so that they do not land in the same hole twice.

The story of AHERF noted the problem of donor-restricted funds that were raided and therefore left as $52.5 million in unfunded liabilities. Not only was this an accounting issue that had to be dealt with in bankruptcy, but the CEO was actually sentenced to prison for diversion of these funds.

Revenue Diversity and Trends

The diversity of revenue sources can reveal much about an organization's long-term financial strength. While virtually all organizations start with one customer, the goal is to diversify the revenue stream as quickly as possible. A $5 million–per-year organization that derives all of its revenue from one customer is both focused and vulnerable. If that same organization had five customers at $1 million each, it would be arguably less vulnerable.

Taking this concept a step further, we assess the multiyear trend in regard to revenue diversity. A new and growing company that increases the scope of its client base and revenue year after year is demonstrating a healthy pattern of revenue diversification. If that diversity includes contrasting markets that each respond differently to economic upturns and downturns, this organization would appear to be less vulnerable to changes in the market environment. Conversely, the corporation with a multiyear trend of fewer and fewer clients may be moving through the Zone of Insolvency.

Nonprofits in the Zone of Insolvency have a tendency to focus on mission while ignoring indicators such as revenue diversity. The reluctance to analyze new trends and take definitive action perpetuates the problem and moves these organizations deeper into the Zone of Insolvency. It is as if they believe that wishful thinking will protect them from the realities of the market environment. But they ignore the trends at their own peril.

PREDICTING FINANCIAL DISTRESS

Modeling to predict financial distress and anticipate bankruptcy has been evolving for over 50 years in the for-profit sector. But predictive modeling for nonprofits is relatively new, and is limited mostly to larger segments such as universities and hospitals. The most significant analysis of nonprofit predictive modeling came out of The Hauser Center for Nonprofit Organizations at Harvard, in a paper titled "Assessing Financial Vulnerability in the Nonprofit Sector" published in 2005.[1] Analyzing the IRS 990 filings for 290,579 nonprofit organizations, the authors tested for financial vulnerability using four key indicators:

1. Insolvency risk
2. Financial disruption
3. Funding disruption
4. Program disruption

On the basis of this sampling, they identified an annual rate of insolvency of 7%, three times the corporate bankruptcy rate for the same period. The highest rate of insolvency was experienced by human services organizations at 10%, followed by healthcare at 7%. The lowest rate of insolvency was in education with a rate of 3.5%. The study concluded that further research in predictive modeling for nonprofits is necessary and that the models successful in predicting financial distress and bankruptcy of for-profit corporations have limited success when applied to the nonprofit sector. (Please note that this study identified 7% of nonprofits as totally insolvent, which is beyond the estimated 30% that are currently in the Zone of Insolvency).

BANKRUPTCY

Conceptually there are two types of bankruptcy: (1) the protective bankruptcy that gives a corporation opportunity to reorganize for future activity and (2) bankruptcy as a means of final dissolution. Typically, Chapter 11 filings are used in an attempt to reorganize, and Chapter 7 filings are used for final dissolution.

Recent bankruptcy filings by the Catholic Church were designed to protect the considerable assets of the church while working through fair settlements with victims, ultimately with the aim that the church would emerge and continue in service.

In February 2007, the Roman Catholic Diocese of San Diego became the fifth diocese in the nation to file for bankruptcy as a result of multiple lawsuits alleging sexual misconduct by priests. Since San Diego is one of the wealthiest dioceses in the nation, the bankruptcy court must now decide whether the filing is a frivolous misuse of bankruptcy law in order to avoid litigation. The federal judge overseeing the bankruptcy proceedings called for an outside accounting expert to sort through what she called "the most Byzantine accounting system I have ever seen," and ordered diocese lawyers and priests to explain why they should not be sanctioned for trying to move church money to new bank accounts, with new identification numbers, without court authorization.[2]

Moral failure in the context of the church strikes at the very heart of the church as teacher of morals. Through the ages, when the church teaches about the cost of immorality, it is traditionally speaking about the human cost. The costs in this story are first human, second organizational, and third financial. Our focus is on the financial.

San Diego's bankruptcy filing follows filings by dioceses in Tucson, Portland, Spokane, and Davenport, Iowa. When the Dallas diocese threatened bankruptcy, litigants settled for one-third of the $119.6 million award determined by the courts, and the diocese then managed to avoid filing for bankruptcy. The Los Angeles Archdiocese agreed to pay victims $60 million without filing for bankruptcy, but hundreds of additional cases are pending. In 2004, the Orange County Diocese paid $100 million without filing for bankruptcy.[3]

This tale has many subplots, winding through the Zone of Insolvency, bankruptcies, plans for workouts, payments to victims who will never be made whole, criminal charges against priests, and devastating image problems for the church.

Board Perspective on the Zone of Insolvency

Even with a complete understanding of the defining issues, individual board members may have differences of opinion regarding an organization's status relative to the Zone of Insolvency. For some, the discussion of the organization's limitations or failures may seem like an attack. Others may simply be more comfortable with denial. Still others believe that their responsibility as board members is to cheer the organization on against all odds. Confession may be good for the soul, but the soul of a board can be tormented when trying to "'fess up" to the reality that their favorite organization is in fact living in the Zone of Insolvency. Failure to deal with the issue and declare that the organization has crossed into the zone of severe financial distress is to miss the opportunity to develop solutions and work deliberately to move out of the zone.

In *Governance as Leadership,* Chait, Ryan, and Taylor suggest that the work of the board is highly episodic, and some work of the board is intrinsically unsatisfying.[4] The board's work in dealing with a financially distressed nonprofit is both episodic and intrinsically unsatisfying. The episodic nature of board work has to do with the rhythm of organizational life cycles. Issues come and go during a typical life cycle, and the board must deal with the current issue or episode. It is natural that all board members would prefer to be dealing with a financially vibrant organization. And because nonprofit board work is typically a volunteer's labor of love for a cause of personal value, the expectation is high that the board work will be intrinsically satisfying. Board members who face an episode of financial distress may find that dealing with issues of insolvency that demand management change, radical reorganization, merger, or even dissolution may be intrinsically unsatisfying.

If the board resolves to break the chains of the Zone of Insolvency and moves the organization to financial viability, there will ultimately be a great sense of satisfaction. But if the board, in its wisdom, proceeds down the path of dissolution, board members may feel that their service was for naught. Does this mean that their service was in vain? Not at all. In fact, if board members begin to view their service on two levels, they will greatly enhance the likelihood of experiencing intrinsic satisfaction. At the primary level, the board is responsible to protect and enhance the assets of the particular organization that they serve. But at the secondary level, they serve as trustees of that great public trust composed of 1.5 million nonprofits with $3 trillion of assets. Following the path of dissolution may be unsatisfying at the primary level, but if it protects and enhances the great public trust, it serves a purpose that may be intrinsically satisfying at the secondary level. Individual organizations will rise and fall, but the real treasure is the combined strength and output of the greater public trust.

FIVE GREAT QUESTIONS FOR YOUR NEXT BOARD MEETING

1. What indications, if any, do we have that suggest that we are in the Zone of Insolvency?
2. Do we have board agreement about where we are positioned on the solvency chart?
3. If we do not have board agreement about where we are positioned, what will it take to adopt a position?
4. If we are in the Zone of Insolvency, how long have we been there?
5. If we are in the Zone of Insolvency, what can we learn from other similar organizations about our options moving forward?

NOTES

1. Elizabeth, Keating, Mary Fischer, Teresa P. Gordon, and Jane Greenlee, "Assessing Financial Vulnerability in the Nonprofit Sector," working paper 27, Hauser Center for Nonprofit Organizations, Harvard University, 2005.
2. Richard, Chait, William Ryans, and Barbara Taylor, *Governance as Leadership.* Hoboken, NJ: John Wiley & Sons, 2005, p. 14.
3. Tony, Perry, "San Diego Diocese Files for Bankruptcy," *Los Angeles Times,* February 28, 2007, section A, p. 1.
4. Ibid.

CHAPTER 12

Governance Risks

Character is built by what you stand for, reputation by what you fall for.

—Anonymous

The legal responsibilities of the board governing an organization in the Zone of Insolvency are expanded from a fiduciary responsibility to protect the assets of the corporation to a broader role of balancing all interests of all parties of the corporation. For the nonprofit organization, this requires balancing the interests of all stakeholders, creditors, funders, customers, and the community at large. Balancing all of these interests can be infinitely more complex than the traditional role of the board. The board that is not aware of its legally expanded responsibilities in the Zone of Insolvency—and does not recognize that it is operating in the Zone of Insolvency—is at considerable risk of unknowingly running afoul of the law and increasing its legal liabilities. Ignorance of the law is not a good legal defense. Law firm Holme Roberts and Owen, LLP articulates the issues of deepening insolvency:

> Although the theory of deepening insolvency has many ambiguities, and arguably does not create a new cause of action, it cannot be ignored so long as the courts continue to apply it. Deepening insolvency claims are typically alleged in connection with fraud or fiduciary duty claims that are brought personally against directors and officers. . . . In addition to

the personal risk of liability, there may be difficulties in obtaining indemnification or director and officer insurance coverage for the legal expenses incurred in defending such claims.[1]

The Zone of Insolvency is a period of severe financial stress during which a corporation may experience dwindling reserves, cash flow problems, and the potential for insolvency. If the potential for actual insolvency is at least foreseeable, a corporation may be deemed to be operating in the Zone of Insolvency. Unfortunately, most nonprofit boards have minimal knowledge of this issue or of its potential for risk.

If a corporation moves from the Zone of Insolvency to total insolvency, options include dissolution, merger, or a workout while under the protection of the U.S. Bankruptcy Code. The U.S. bankruptcy laws have been in constant evolution since the very first bankruptcy law was passed in 1800. During the nineteenth century, Congress passed three different bankruptcy laws, and each one was repealed within 11 years or less. Each of these laws, was a response to the general economic stresses of the day, focusing on protections for creditors. "[A] Delaware Chancery Court's footnote in *Credit Lyonnais Bank Nederland NV v. Pathe Communications,* 1991 WL 277613 (Del. Ch. 1991), established the 'Zone of Insolvency' as something to be feared by directors and officers and served as a catalyst for countless creditor lawsuits. Claims by creditors, committees, and trustees, against directors, and officers, for breach of fiduciary duties owed to creditors, have since become commonplace."[2]

In the twentieth century, bankruptcy laws began to offer protections for individuals and corporations. Ultimately they evolved to provide protection for the entity while reorganizing or working out debt. They also created an orderly process for dissolution, with rules for disbursement of remaining assets when liabilities exceed assets. The end of the twentieth century was marked by a steep increase in the numbers of corporate bankruptcies, accompanied by the growth in the number of professionals specializing in bankruptcy law, liquidations, and workouts.[3]

The Zone of Insolvency was first identified in the 1991 ruling by the Delaware Chancery Court in *Credit Lyonnais Bank Nederland NV v. Pathe Communications.* The court identified the potential for directors and officers to be held liable for fiduciary decisions while in the Zone of Insolvency.[4] Prior to this ruling, it was always held that boards were responsible solely to the corporation and its shareholders, not to creditors or other stakeholders. In its ruling in this case, the court stated,

> When a company enters the Zone of Insolvency, its directors owe fiduciary duties to creditors and other members of the corporate enterprise, as well as to shareholders. Certain actions to be avoided for which directors could be held personally liable when the company is in the zone of insolvency include failing to pay taxes, failing to pay wages, paying dividends to shareholders, sales or transfers for inadequate consideration, and violating duties under ERISA. Delaware requires directors of a company in the zone of insolvency to consider the effect on creditors of any proposed transaction. In contrast, the Minnesota courts, to date, have tended to find directors of a financially distressed company personally liable to creditors only for transactions that involve self-dealing or insider preferences. Whether a director actually will be liable for any of these actions depends on state law. Also, indemnification arrangements and D&O insurance may be available to provide some protection for directors depending on the basis for liability. Directors of a financially distressed company should seek advice as to their duties under the law of the state in which the company is incorporated. Following good business practices, as described above, is key to avoiding director and officer liability.[5]

So we enter the twenty-first century with new legal precedent and case law demonstrating that boards governing corporations in the Zone of Insolvency assume expanded responsibilities. Attorneys at Dorsey & Whitney, LLP, point out that as corporations approach insolvency, the responsibilities of the board are expanded to include the interests of creditors and the entire corporate enterprise.[6]

Since the Delaware Chancery Court's ruling in *Credit Lyonnais Bank,* case law has evolved to apply the Zone of Insolvency to nonprofit organizations as well. The case of the Allegheny Health, Education and Research Foundation makes it clear that nonprofit boards must pay greater attention to the Zone of Insolvency and act prudently in the interest of all parties as their organizations experience great financial stress.[7] Attorneys at Vedder Price indicate that if a corporation is in severe financial distress, the courts will generally find that the corporation was in the Zone of Insolvency, thereby opening the door to scrutinize board actions to assure that they acted in good faith and honored their fiduciary responsibilities to all appropriate parties of interest.[8]

BOARD REVIEW PROCESS

The prudent board constantly monitors organizational performance and status, but when governing in the Zone of Insolvency, it is critical that the board be extraordinarily diligent about such reviews. There are numerous components, discussed in the following text, that should be factored into board reviews. Such reviews should incorporate regular, methodical, documented monitoring that measures performance against board policies and expectations. Without documentation of such activity while governing in the Zone of Insolvency, a board could readily be labeled as fiscally irresponsible. Adequate director's and officer's liability insurance is critical when governing in the zone, although it does not protect board members for criminal acts or pay off debt in the event of dissolution.

Balance Statement

An ongoing assessment of assets versus liabilities is a critical measure that should always be under constant review by the board, especially when in financial distress. Gone are the days when board members can proclaim that they do not have the financial background to comment on balance sheets. The liabilities involved with sitting on a nonprofit board are too high. Every board member must take the initiative to learn how to read the financial statements and actively engage in review. Every board member should be able to read a balance statement and draw a reasonable conclusion regarding the corporation's status relative to the Zone of Insolvency. And every board member should be able to answer the question "How much would dissolution cost?" Assuming that the board would not want to see creditors accrue loss through dissolution, the board should be very aware of the net assets relative to any possibility of dissolution.

Benchmark Reports

The board that takes the time to establish benchmarks and insists on regular benchmark reports from management demonstrates diligence while in the Zone of Insolvency. Ideally these benchmarks would be based on comparisons with the performance of similar organizations. At a minimum, the benchmarks can be internal performance standards based on previous performance and environmental changes. When management achieves the benchmark, minimal additional detail is needed by the board. When management misses the benchmark, the board will naturally need to probe deeper into the details for a more complete understanding of the problem.

Budgeting

The board must hold management responsible for meeting budget expectations, especially in times of severe financial distress. Actual versus budget variances should be explained in detail, with plans to get back on budget. Budget must be realistic and achievable. By investing the time to build a sound budget up front, management can meet or exceed expectations and rebuild board confidence. Failure to achieve budget expectations in a financially distressed corporation will quickly erode board confidence. As the board struggles to meet its fiduciary responsibilities in the Zone of Insolvency, it will have little tolerance for budget variances. Surprisingly, significant positive variances may diminish board confidence as much as negative variances, because both leave the board feeling out of control.

Capital Acquisitions or Disposal

Capital acquisition or disposal while in the Zone of Insolvency holds high potential for litigation. Extraordinary care must be taken to assure that all such transactions are fair and fairly priced so as not to disadvantage any particular stakeholder group. For example, a quick sale of real estate at a price well below fair market value may solve a cash flow problem at the expense of creditors who may not be paid in full or in a timely fashion. Extraordinary caution should be used to avoid any perception or reality of insider deals in regard to liquidation of assets.

Cash Flow Management

When operating in the Zone of Insolvency, the acceptable margin for error is reduced as cash reserves are reduced. As a result, cash flow management is most critical during this period and must be reviewed regularly by the board. Inability to meet payroll or payables due to cash flow irregularities will not be well received by a board sensitive to its fiduciary responsibilities in the Zone of Insolvency. Just as with budget variances, cash flow problems will leave the board feeling that management has lost control and will put the board at greater risk.

Contracts and Leases

Board review of all new contracts and leases is critical while operating in the Zone of Insolvency. Signing or renewing a lease or contract while in severe financial distress may result in a loss to creditors if the organization is unable to meet its financial obligations. The board that allows or authorizes new contracts or leases while in the Zone of Insolvency may find that it is liable for actions that did not give due consideration to the rights of creditors. This does not mean that contracts or leases can never be signed while in financial distress, but every effort must be taken to assure fairness and open disclosure with all related parties.

Debt

Monitoring debt levels is critical to understanding the condition of the organization and anticipating trends indicating deepening financial distress or a turnaround. Constantly increasing debt may be cause for concern, especially in view of the debt ratio. Debt management may prove critical to cash flow management. If the corporation's line of credit is maxed out and cash reserves are depleted, any irregularities in cash flow may prove catastrophic. Establishing appropriate benchmarks is critical to monitoring debt ratios, gross debt, and available lines of credit.

Executive Compensation

Executive compensation, especially performance bonuses or salary increases, must be carefully scrutinized when operating in the Zone of Insolvency. Rewarding executives at a time when creditors are being paid late, or not at all, is particularly risky for a board governing a financially distressed organization. On the other hand, a more experienced executive who demands a higher salary may bring better skills and increase the likelihood of a successful turnaround. It is critical that compensation decisions be based on rates in comparable organizations, not just the internal feelings of the board.

Loans to Employees or Board

While loans to employees or board are typically ill advised, they are highly likely to trigger litigation when operating in the Zone of Insolvency. Self-dealing or conflict of interest must be strictly avoided. Boards that find that they have inherited such loans should work with legal counsel to transition such loans to outside parties as quickly as possible and should introduce policies to assure that such loans are not offered again.

Payables

During times of severe financial distress, management may be tempted or forced to delay payment of payables. Monitoring increases in payables is critical to diligent governance. Special attention should be focused on timely payment of taxes, Social Security, and pension contributions to assure compliance with state and federal law. The board must demand absolute transparency from management in regard to all reporting on the status of payables and must understand any timing issues between reports of payables and actual payment of payables. If management defers payment of payroll taxes or employee benefits, it may be in violation of federal or state laws, and the board could be liable for these violations in addition to any general fiduciary failures related to the Zone of Insolvency.

Performance Reviews

A prudent board must constantly monitor executive performance to determine whether an executive is part of the problem or part of the solution when it comes to governing a financially distressed organization. Documenting executive performance is an essential board obligation, in keeping with the board's fiduciary responsibility. Nonprofit boards are typically reluctant to make changes, and many are arguably soft on performance compared with the for-profit sector. But if an executive is the cause for financial failure or is not capable of successfully negotiating a turnaround, it may be argued that by tolerating that executive, a board failed in its fiduciary responsibilities.

Receivables

Aging receivables may be an indicator of management problems in a financially distressed organization and may even be used by management to inflate assets and mask the true financial picture. By carrying aged receivables that should have been written off, the assets may be inflated to balance against liabilities. When governing an organization in the Zone of Insolvency, a board must exhibit a healthy degree of skepticism and closely monitor the status of receivables. The board should have a policy that clearly establishes expectations for management of receivables and should regularly monitor for compliance with this policy.

Restricted and Designated Funds

Nonprofit organizations typically manage donor-restricted and board designated funds set aside for special purposes. The diligent board will have policies strictly controlling use of these funds and forbidding borrowing against these restricted funds. Monitoring these funds during times of financial distress is particularly important. While it may not be required by generally accepted accounting procedures, some organizations will find it prudent to maintain restricted and designated funds in accounts separate from general operating funds to assure that there is never any inadvertent internal borrowing against these funds. Failure to comply with requirements for government grants may be a violation of state or federal law, complete with fines or jail time for board and management in addition to typical issues of fiduciary responsibility in the Zone of Insolvency.

Self-Dealing

Self-dealing is never appropriate behavior for a nonprofit board or management. When operating in the Zone of Insolvency, with the expanded board responsibilities for creditors and stakeholders, any appearance of self-dealing may well draw the ire of creditors and trigger litigation against board members individually and corporately. For an organization to have a board member who is also a vendor or creditor can be particularly problematic, whether as a consultant, insurance agent, printer, or something else. While most nonprofit boards do not compensate board members, extraordinary care should be given to compensation, board gifts, or board entertainment and travel while governing in the Zone of Insolvency. Gracious gifts and entertainment that may have been an accepted part of a board culture for years should be reconsidered, especially when nearing the Zone of Insolvency.

Securing Fairness Opinions

While it is always prudent for a board to obtain a fairness opinion when making a major financial decision, this is especially important when operating in the Zone of Insolvency. The fairness opinion is an independent analysis that offers an objective opinion regarding a proposed deal, such as a sale of property. Prior to agreeing to a deal, the board is well advised to obtain the independent fairness ruling to assure that no other stakeholder will second-guess the decision. This is especially important if there are creditors who are not being paid because of the severe financial stress of the organization, as those creditors will want to verify that a fair price was obtained in return for sale of property. A legitimate fairness opinion will go a long way in protecting directors from any personal liability arising from allegations of an unfair deal.

Delegation

Sound governance requires boards to establish policies, define a direction, and delegate responsibility for implementation to the executive team. When governing in the Zone of Insolvency, the board must constantly review executive performance to assure compliance with board policies and implementation of board directives. If challenged by creditors or stakeholders, the board will find that delegating responsibility for implementation is not a solid defense unless they are also monitoring for compliance.

Balancing Mission and Finances

Nonprofits are constantly challenged to balance commitment to mission with a need to protect and enhance the fiscal viability of the organization. On one hand, there is a desire to show compassion rather than being driven solely by business solutions and money. On the other hand, if the organization is not fiscally viable, it will not survive to implement and expand the mission. This balance typically shifts from one side to the other as an organization evolves, but shifts dramatically to the finance side when in the Zone of Insolvency. The board must honor the mission, even in dissolution. But honoring mission with reckless abandon to core fiduciary responsibilities puts the corporation and board members individually at great risk. Never has this been as true as it is today.

BOARD/MANAGEMENT TENSIONS IN THE ZONE OF INSOLVENCY

In an article in the *American Bankruptcy Institute Journal* (2002), authors Heather Kaplan and Michael Peregrine state:

> The recent settlement in Allegheny Health, Education and Research Foundation (AHERF) relating to the recovery of allegedly misapplied charitable assets, together with the general fragility of the health care finance system, suggests that fiduciaries of health industry companies should be—and are increasingly being advised by sophisticated health care attorneys and financial advisors to be attentive to "Zone of Insolvency" issues when they encounter financial distress. While compliance with the Sarbanes-Oxley Act should make the corporate board more attentive to financial oversight, the "shift" in a director's fiduciary duties (for the benefit of creditors) that occurs when a corporation becomes insolvent is unlikely to be readily apparent to the board (regardless of its diligence). This may be particularly so for the many health industry companies that are not-for-profits with "charitable missions" (i.e., no shareholders) and whose boards are generally composed of community representatives. Yet Zone-of-Insolvency concepts, which have been applied to commercial ventures for years, are becoming increasingly relevant to such health industry companies. Unfamiliarity with those duties in the Zone of Insolvency can create problems for the board and for its creditors.[9]

While attention to details in these areas is always prudent, it takes on a completely new level of significance when governing in the Zone of Insolvency. Given the evolving legal emphasis on corporate responsibility and accountability in governance, boards face ever increasing liabilities when governing severely financially distressed organizations. As a result, boards must be more diligent about avoiding the Zone of Insolvency and pursuing every means of working out of the zone, or merging, or pursuing dissolution (see Exhibit 12.1).

But as the board becomes more engaged in these issues, the relationship between management and board will experience significant stress. Executives may be confused by the board's new level of attention to areas previously delegated to management. And the board, concerned about the Zone of Insolvency, will find itself evaluating management performance.

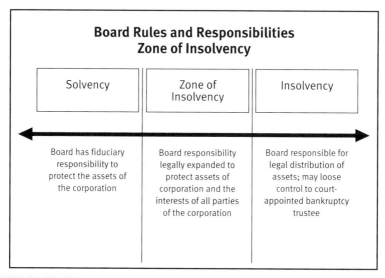

EXHIBIT 12.1   BOARD ROLES AND RESPONSIBILITIES

It will likely feel uncertainty regarding whom it should trust to restore and rebuild fiscal viability—that is, is management part of the problem or part of the solution? Building board alignment around performance evaluations is critical to moving ahead to constructive resolution. The board may be so preoccupied with finances that it appears to lose focus on the mission, creating additional stresses on board/management relationships. Finally, if the board finds it necessary to consider dissolution, merger, or filing for bankruptcy, it may find that management takes a very defensive stance and depicts the board as not committed to the mission. A 2004 publication by the law firm of Vedder Price stated:

> In general, if a corporation is in dire financial straits, a court will likely find that the corporation is in the zone of insolvency. Accordingly, when a corporation is in financial distress, its directors and officers should assume that they are in the zone of insolvency, and should be making decisions and taking actions on the basis that they owe fiduciary duties to creditors as well as stockholders. However, by ensuring that all transactions involving the corporation are entered into in good faith, are fair and reasonable, and without self-dealing or favoritism toward any group of stakeholders, directors should be able to navigate their duties in the zone of insolvency with few difficulties.[10]

FIVE GREAT QUESTIONS FOR YOUR NEXT BOARD MEETING

1. Do we understand our individual and corporate liabilities while governing a nonprofit corporation in the Zone of Insolvency?
2. Do we understand our director's and officer's liability insurance, and can we identify areas where we may have uninsured liability as a board members?
3. Have we identified our expanded responsibilities as a board governing a nonprofit in the Zone of Insolvency?
4. If we are governing an organization in the Zone of Insolvency, are we diligently reviewing management's performance indicators to minimize our liabilities?
5. If we are governing in the Zone of Insolvency, do we have a turn-around plan to work away from the zone, arrange a merger, or file for dissolution?

SAMPLE BOARD POLICIES FOR AVOIDING OR ESCAPING THE ZONE OF INSOLVENCY

The following sample policies are intended to provoke thought but should not be adapted word for word, because each organization's needs are unique. It may be helpful to review your organization's existing policy book, contemplate current issues, and identify areas where you need to add policies or revise existent policies.

Policy Governing Review of Grants and Proposals

It is our policy that the board of directors must give prior approval for any grant application or program proposal that would account for "10"% or more of the annual revenue of the corporation.

Policy Governing Conflict of Interest

Board members shall avoid any and all conflicts of interest that could occur when they are in a position to influence decisions that may result in a personal gain for themselves, or for a relative, as a result of this organization's business dealings. Any board member that has influence on transactions involving purchases, contracts, or leases shall immediately disclose the potential for conflict to an officer of the corporation.

Policy Governing Consulting Fees

It is our policy that no individual serving on the board of directors shall receive a fee, salary, or commission for providing consulting or business services to the organization.

Policy Governing Fund Balance

The reserve balance of the net assets shall be maintained above a minimum of "50"% of the annual revenues of the organization with no maximum. If the net assets drop below the "50"% level required by this policy, the Executive Director is to notify the board and immediately present a plan to reduce expenses and restore the net assets to the "50"% minimum level.

Policy Governing Expenditures

We hereby delegate to the Executive Director full responsibility to exercise adequate internal controls over receipts and disbursements and to avoid unauthorized payments or material dissipation of assets. The Executive Director shall not allow the development of fiscal jeopardy, or a material deviation of actual expenditures from the board's priorities.

Policy Governing Unbudgeted Expenditures

It is our intent that this board shall demonstrate restraint and self-discipline in regard to unbudgeted expenses. Therefore, it is our policy that the board shall adjust budgets or identify additional funding to cover unbudgeted board expenditures prior to authorization.

Policy Governing Pricing Policy

We hereby delegate to the Executive Director the responsibility to set prices, and it is our expectation that those prices will honor the mission of the organization and protect the fiscal viability of the organization.

Management shall not obligate the organization to any contracts that do not cover all direct costs while contributing to the payment of indirect overheads, and shall terminate all contracts that do not cover both direct and indirect expenses.

Any proposed contract that falls short of covering all direct and indirect expenses may be subsidized through fundraising, but only if the funds are raised prior to the initiation of service.

Policy Governing Borrowing of Funds

It is our policy that the borrowing of funds, increasing of indebtedness, or otherwise increasing of the line of credit shall require authorization of the board.

Policy Governing Board-Designated Funds

Board-designated funds shall be maintained in separate accounts from general operating cash and may not be borrowed against or otherwise used for any purpose other than the board-designated intent.

Policy Governing Donor-Restricted Funds

It is our policy that donor-restricted funds shall be officially accepted by the corporation only after the board approves a written copy of donor intent. Donor-restricted funds shall be maintained in separate accounts from general operating cash and may not be borrowed against or otherwise used for any purpose other than the original donor-specified intent.

Policy Governing Payroll, Tax Filing, and Retirement Funds Obligations

We hereby delegate to the Executive Director full responsibility to settle payroll obligations, tax filings, 990s, and retirement funds distributions on time and in accord with all appropriate state and federal regulations.

Policy Governing Payables

It is our policy and expectation that the Executive Director shall make every effort to pay all payables within "30" days, and shall at no time

extend payables beyond "60" days without informing the Board Treasurer in writing.

Policy Governing Purchase Authorizations

We hereby delegate authority to the Executive Director to execute checks or purchase commitments up to [$50,000] unless such purchase was explicitly itemized in the board-approved budget or otherwise approved in writing by the board. Splitting orders to avoid this limit is not acceptable.

Policy Governing Acquisition and Disposal of Real Property

It is our policy that the Executive Director shall not acquire, encumber, lease, or dispose of real property with value in excess of $50,000 without approval of the board.

Policy Governing Receivables

It is our policy and expectation that the Executive Director shall aggressively pursue material receivables after a 30-day grace period. All receivables in excess of 90 days shall be reviewed monthly with the Board Treasurer, who shall take every reasonable measure to minimize carrying doubtful receivables on the books as assets, in keeping with generally accepted accounting principles.

Five Great Questions for Your Next Board Meeting

1. Does this board have adequate policy governing acquisition and disposal of property?
2. Do we start off every board meeting with a review of our policy on conflict of interest?
3. Do we have adequate policy to assure review of charitable gifts terms prior to acceptance of major gifts?
4. Are we as an organization pricing strategically?
5. Does this board have an adequate understanding of the true valve of our receivables?

Notes

1. Holme Roberts & Owen LLP, "Avoiding the Undertow of Deepening Insolvency," August 12, 2005, Denver.
2. Allen, Kadish and Luis Salazar, "Delaware Chancery Court Takes Fresh Look at 'Zone of Insolvency,'" *New York Law Journal,* vol. 233, no. 57 (2005), pp. 1–2.
3. *The 2001 Bankruptcy Yearbook and Almanac.* Boston: New Generation Research, Inc., 2001.
4. Kadish and Salazar, "Delaware Chancery Court Takes Fresh Look at 'Zone of Insolvency.'"
5. Dorsey & Whitney, LLP, "Fiduciary Duties and the Zone of Insolvency—*Pereira v. Cogan* Reminds Directors of Private Corporations of Their Duties to Shareholders and Creditors," October 2003.
6. Ibid.
7. Heather, Kaplan and Michael Peregrine, "Healthcare Enters the Zone of Insolvency," *American Bankruptcy Institute Journal,* vol. 22, no. 8 (2002), pp. 1–2.
8. "Directors' Duties in the Zone of Insolvency: A Practical Guide," Vedder Price, 2004.
9. Kaplan and Peregrine, "Healthcare Enters the Zone of Insolvency."
10. "Directors' Duties in the Zone of Insolvency."

PART THREE

Symptoms

Part of understanding any disease is identifying common symptoms. A better understanding of the symptoms enables us to more readily identify the disease in a patient and to anticipate the life cycle of the disease. In the case of nonprofit organizations there are symptoms common to financially strong organizations and other symptoms common to financially distressed organizations. There is much to be learned from each.

CHAPTER 13

Fundraising Hazards

Tell those who are rich not to be proud and not to trust in their money, which will soon be gone. . . . Tell them to use their money to do good. They should be rich in good works and should give happily to those in need, always being ready to share with others whatever God has given them.

—1 TIMOTHY 6: 17–19 (LIVING BIBLE)

Americans give over $260 billion per year in charitable gifts, fueling the engines of a nonprofit community with annual gross expenditures greater than the gross national product of Russia. Responding to major natural disasters between December 2004 and October 2005, Americans gave an astounding $7 billion for disaster relief in less than 12 months.[1] Over 90% of U.S. households have donated to charity in the past year, but one-third of U.S. adults have less than positive feelings toward charitable organizations, and only 1 in 10 believes that charitable organizations are honest and ethical in their use of funds.[2] Two of the key reasons that people state for not giving are that they do not believe the money is used efficiently, and they believe that charities have become too much like for-profits.[3]

No discussion of nonprofit organizations is complete without consideration of the role of charitable giving. The moral mandate to give can be traced back to ancient cultures and to the teachings of most major religions; in earlier times, alms and gifts of food, water, clothing, or shelter were offered directly to the needy. Today's giving is more sanitized, with donors sending checks to charities that provide the delivery of services directly to those in need. As a result, today's donor rarely deals directly with the needy recipient of the gift but rather gives to the organization deemed most effective and most trustworthy in their delivery of services. Although over 90% of households have made charitable gifts in the past year, few of these gift givers dealt directly by giving food, shelter, or clothing to the homeless.

In this environment, institutional integrity is the foundation for fundraising success. If prospective donors do not trust the organization, they will not give, regardless of the quality or urgency of the appeal. When it comes to evaluating fundraising appeals by financially distressed organizations, a bit of skepticism will serve donors well. The Donor Bill of Rights, as developed by the Association of Fundraising Professionals, identifies 10 specific rights of donors, the first four of which are pertinent to our considerations:

1. The right to be informed of the organization's mission, of the way the organization intends to use donated resources, and of its capacity to use donations effectively for their intended purposes
2. The right to be informed of the identity of those serving on the organization's governing board, and to expect the board to exercise prudent judgment in its stewardship responsibilities
3. The right to have access to the organization's most recent financial statements
4. The right to be assured that their gifts will be used for the purposes for which they were given

Consider these four rights in light of some of the tales related chapters 1–10. In the United Way/Aramony tale, the donors' rights to expect prudent stewardship by the board were violated by extravagant and unlawful expenditures by management. In the New Era/Bennett tale, donors' rights were violated by failure to identify names of board members, failure to provide financial statements, failure of the board to exercise prudent stewardship, and the ultimate reality that gifts were not used for the intended purpose (again the issue of extravagant and unlawful expenditures by management). In the tale of AHERF/Abdelhak, the violation of donor rights was particularly egregious with $52.5 million raided from donor-restricted funds and lost forever in the depths of bankruptcy.

We focus in this chapter on the challenges of raising funds for financially distressed nonprofit organizations that may or may not be in the Zone of

Insolvency. Every fundraiser understands the value of urgency in an appeal. As an organization moves into the Zone of Insolvency, the urgent appeal can cast a shadow over the commitment to transparency, placing the integrity of the organization at risk. The tightrope walked by the fundraiser demands transparency about the true financial condition of the organization, within the context of the urgent appeal. There are a number of weighty issues that can throw the fundraiser off balance in the midst of that tightrope walk.

DONOR-RESTRICTED GIFTS

Consider, for a moment, the fundraiser for a nonprofit that is operating in the Zone of Insolvency. The board, executive team, and staff all have high expectations that the fundraiser can save the day with extraordinary talent and perhaps a bit of good luck. A major donor is determined to give a large designated gift. The designation restricts the use of the funds to a long-term capital need but does nothing to solve the immediate cash flow problems. The fundraiser has tried to convince the donor to redirect the gift to address the more urgent cash flow crisis, but the donor will not reconsider.

Q1: If the organization accepts the gift but subsequently files for dissolution and/or bankruptcy, did it violate the rights of the donor?
A1: Yes, if the organization was not perfectly clear about the dire financial condition of the organization. No, if the donor clearly understood the risks and chose to give anyway.
Q2: Could the organization accept the capital gift, book it, but then borrow the funds internally to solve the cash flow crisis?
A2: No. The donor has a right to be assured that the gift will be used for the intended purpose. To assure this right, the gift should be separately invested, not commingled with general operating cash. There should be board policy governing such a transaction.

ANNUITIES

Charitable gift annuities issued by nonprofit organizations can pose serious challenges in the event of dissolution and/or bankruptcy. Commercially issued annuities are highly regulated by the SEC, but surprisingly, most states allow nonprofit organizations to issue annuities without any requirement that they hold and protect the principal. The simple gift annuity begins with a lump-sum payment from the annuitant to the nonprofit organization. The nonprofit then commits to a payment schedule for the life of the annuitant—in essence, an interest payment. At the death of the annuitant the nonprofit keeps the principal as a gift. While best practice would suggest that the non-profit protect and invest the principal until the death of the annuitant, this is not required by law in most states. This can become a significant issue for the nonprofit in financial distress. If it strips the principal before the death of the annuitant and still has an obligation for the schedule of payments, the annuitant may end up as a creditor in the event of bankruptcy.

Q1: Is a nonprofit required to protect and invest the principal of an annuity until the death of the annuitant?

A1: Check with legal counsel regarding requirements in your state. In most states it is not required by law, but it is certainly recommended as best practice.

Q2: Does the donor have a right to know how the principal will be handled during the life of the annuitant?

A2: Absolutely.

Donors as Creditors in Bankruptcy

Nobody likes to consider the possibility of dissolution or bankruptcy—or worse yet, the disposition of the donors in such a case. Generally speaking, donors have given to an organization, and the organization now has fiduciary responsibility. If the donor asks the nonprofit to return the funds, there may be some legal hurdles to jump to assure that the fiduciary responsibility of the board is not violated by the return. In the event of a bankruptcy, the donors may not be considered unless they ask for consideration. For instance, a donor who gave a designated gift may argue that the funds were never spent on the intended purpose and may appeal to the bankruptcy trustee for return of the funds. If the trustee approves the request, it is most likely that the donor would then be listed with the other general unsecured creditors. After all of the higher-priority creditors are paid off, the remaining assets are distributed proportionately between the general unsecured creditors, who may receive pennies on the dollar.

Consider the tale in Chapter 1 about the nonprofit organizations and philanthropists who were defrauded by New Era/Bennett. The bankruptcy trustee worked to recover funds from the settlement with Prudential Securities and to recover the "profits" distributed by New Era to some of the participating organizations in order to restore, at least in part, the losses incurred by the victims—that is, the creditors.

Q1: Are the donors automatically creditors in a bankruptcy?

A1: Not necessarily. Unless donors file an appeal with the bankruptcy trustee for return of gifts, it is doubtful that they would be recognized at all.

Hiring Fundraisers in the Zone of Insolvency

The story is all too common. A nonprofit in financial distress decides that the cure is a desperation attempt at fundraising. They roll the dice and risk the remaining few dollars to hire a fundraiser. The fundraiser soon realizes that there are no funds to support the fundraising activities and that unless funds are raised immediately, even salary will be in jeopardy. It usually fails. It's like trying to make pickles by sprinkling vinegar on a cucumber. Fundraising demands an investment of time and resources, and the "Hail Mary" pass rarely works. The fundraiser will find it difficult to share the urgency of the situation without painting such a negative picture of the organization that donors will be scared off. And the fundraiser, realizing that salary money is dependent on the unlikely prospect of instant success, will likely be looking for another job.

Over the long haul, fundraisers should be able to raise at a minimum two or three times their salary, but this will not be the case during the first two years. The prudent board will view the first two years of a fundraiser's salary and expenses as an investment, not as instant profit. Finally, the fundraiser in this situation may find it increasingly difficult to comply with a traditional fundraiser's code of ethics. For instance, the Code of Ethical Principles and Standards of Professional Practice for the Association of Fundraising Professionals states that "members shall not engage in activities that conflict with their fiduciary, ethical and legal obligations to their organizations and to their clients."[4]

COMMISSIONS FOR FUNDRAISERS

A great temptation for financially distressed nonprofits is to hire a fundraiser on commission to reduce the risk of salary without performance. This is ill advised on all counts, and the fundraiser who would agree to such an arrangement should never be hired, for any other reason than his or her willingness to accept this unethical arrangement. The Code of Ethics for the Association of Fundraising Professionals states that "members shall not accept compensation that is based on a percentage of charitable contributions, nor shall they accept finder's fees." Commission-based compensation for fundraisers leaves the fundraiser in the untenable position of coaxing larger and larger gifts out of donors for his or her own personal benefit.

TRANSFERRING DONATIONS THROUGH MULTIPLE CORPORATE ENTITIES

Remember the tale of AHERF/Abdlhak in Chapter 3? At the point of bankruptcy there were multiple boards, multiple legal entities, multiple audits, general confusion about all of the funds transfers, and $52.5 million of charitable gifts missing. In the 1980s, a nonprofit religious publisher established a U.S corporation and separate corporations on each continent. American donors were solicited by the U.S. corporation to give gifts designated for specific projects overseas. But the funds never went to the designated projects, and the audits were for the U.S. corporation only. When challenged to explain the final disposition of funds, executives stated that the obligation of the U.S. corporation was to raise the funds and forward them to the appropriate international corporation noting the donor designations. The international corporations were free to use the funds as they saw fit; there were no audits of the international organizations, and the donors had no recourse. Needless to say, donors found this outcome to be unsatisfactory, and the organization was soon out of business.

Financially stressed nonprofits are sometimes inclined to mask the scope of their problems by transfers through multiple entities. Remember the story of the Baptist Foundation of Arizona in Chapter 6? At the point of bankruptcy they had created over 90 legal entities that ultimately shielded the insolvency from the auditors.

Grants

Another area often seen as a potential instant panacea for the financially distressed nonprofit is grants from either government or foundations. But as every grant writer can tell you, grant proposals are very detailed, and funders scrutinize the financial status of the organization in addition to reviewing the purpose for the grant. In issuing a grant, foundations and government are looking for a "return on investment," at least in the sense of a contribution to society. The grant writer, who in unbridled enthusiasm shades the truth about the financial distress, may face charges of fraud or perjury. And the organization that uses grant funds for other unapproved purposes may also face criminal charges. The board that is governing a nonprofit in the Zone of Insolvency should pay special attention to grant requests to make certain that such applications are truthful, and do not make promises that cannot be kept.

When it comes to fundraising for an organization in the Zone of Insolvency, the board is well advised to consider its legal responsibilities as Duty of Care, Duty of Loyalty, and Duty of Obedience. Duty of Care requires reasonable care and prudent stewardship. Duty of Loyalty requires the avoidance of personal gain or conflict of interest as a trustee puts the organization's needs first. Duty of Obedience demands faithfulness to the mission. Also remember that when governing in the Zone of Insolvency, the legal responsibilities of the board are expanded to include the interests of all parties of the organization, including donors, creditors, stakeholders, patients, students, staff, and the community at large.

Five Great Questions for Your Next Board Meeting

1. Do we as a board have adequate policies in place regarding the receiving, investing, and disbursement of donor-restricted funds?
2. Do we have a board policy regarding review and acceptance of major gifts and donor-restricted gifts?
3. Are our restricted funds balances separately invested and fully funded, or are those funds commingled with general operating reserves?

4. Do we have a policy for internal borrowing against restricted funds?

5. What is our policy and practice regarding donor-restricted funds that have been on the books but cannot now be honored as originally intended by the donor?

Notes

1. *Giving USA Yearbook of Philanthropy,* Giving USA, 2005.
2. The Harris Interactive DonorPulse Survey, January 2006.
3. "Reasons for Not Giving," from Giving and Volunteering in the United States, a national survey by the Independent Sector, 2001.
4. Association of Fundraising Professionals, Code of Ethical Principles and Standards of Professional Practice, adopted 1964; amended 2004.

CHAPTER 14

Dissolution Issues

For-profit dissolution is simple. Not-for-profits, however, must jump through numerous hoops, including obtaining various approvals. Undoubtedly many of the approximately 50,000 not-for-profits currently registered with the New York Department of Law are defunct, but the procedural requirements were simply too daunting for them to follow.

—DAVID W. LOWDEN, *New York Law Journal,* 2006

Jeffrey T. Even, Deputy Solicitor General of Washington, describing his state's process for nonprofit dissolution: (see Exhibit 14.1), asserted, "Washington law requires that before dissolving, any nonprofit corporation that holds assets restricted to charitable uses submit a plan of distribution of assets to the Attorney General." The plan is to describe how the assets will be distributed to other charities, after the payment of all creditors. Attorney General approval (or failing that, judicial approval) is required prior to dissolution. Nonprofit charters always stipulate that in the event of dissolution, any remaining assets must be contributed to another nonprofit. The logic of nontaxable corporations serving the public good requires that the assets never be accrued or disbursed for the benefit of any individuals or for-profit corporations. From the public policy perspective, the community of 1,500,000 nonprofit organizations with combined net assets of $3 trillion is a national treasure, growing stronger for the public good. When a nonprofit organization ceases operations and redistributes remaining net assets within the nonprofit community, the national treasure is perpetuated.

EXHIBIT 14.1   COMPLEXITIES OF NONPROFIT DISSOLUTION

STATE of WASHINGTON   *SECRETARY of STATE*

ARTICLES OF DISSOLUTION
WASHINGTON NONPROFIT CORPORATION ACT
RCW 24.03.240

UBI #: _____

Phone #: _____

Pursuant to the provisions of RCW 24.03.240   the undersigned does hereby submit an application for Articles of Dissolution.

1. The name of the Corporation is: _____
    _____

2. Check and complete one of the following statements:

    ☐ Date of the meeting at which time the members adopted the resolution to dissolve the corporation was _____ 20___.
    A quorum was present at the meeting, and the resolution received at least two-thirds of the votes which members present at the meeting or represented by proxy were entitled to cast.

    ☐ Resolution was adopted by consent in writing signed by all members entitled to vote with respect thereto on _____,20___.

    ☐ There are no members, or no members having voting rights. Therefore, a meeting was held by the board of directors on _____,20___ at which time a resolution was adopted by a majority vote of the directors in office to dissolve the corporation.

3. All debts, obligations, and liabilities of the corporation have been paid and discharged or adequate provision has been made thereof.

4. **Attached is a copy of a revenue clearance certificate issued by the Department of Revenue.**

5. All remaining property and assets of the corporation have been transferred, conveyed or distributed in accordance with the provisions of the law.

6. There are no suits pending against the corporation in any court, or adequate provision has been made for the satisfaction of any judgment, order or decree which may be entered against it in any pending suit.

7. This document is hereby executed under penalties of perjury, and is, to the best of my knowledge true and correct.

    Dated: _____.20___.

    X_____
    (Signature of Officer)

    005-006 (2/96)

Available online at www.secstate.wa.gov/corps/forms

For-profit corporations can be forced involuntarily into bankruptcy by creditors calling for payment and demanding a court-approved orderly process to assure fairness. The legal process of determining who gets paid first and of dividing up remaining assets to pay off creditors, even if it is pennies on the dollar, is best handled by an independent court-appointed trustee.

For-profit corporations can also voluntarily elect bankruptcy, putting themselves under the protection of the courts to arrange for an orderly dissolution, or to attempt a workout. By filing under Chapter 7, the corporation pursues a "turn-key closedown" in which the court-appointed bankruptcy trustee takes over and assures fair distribution of remaining assets between creditors. Under Chapter 11 filings, the organization has protection provided by the bankruptcy courts while it tries to reorganize and work itself out of financial distress.

Nonprofit corporations cannot be forced involuntarily into bankruptcy. They may voluntarily elect bankruptcy, putting themselves under the protection of the courts to arrange for an orderly dissolution or to attempt a workout. But given that nonprofits rely heavily on goodwill and charitable donations, workouts are generally problematic, as they tend to erode goodwill and diminish the potential for future success in fundraising. For this reason, Chapter 11 filings are not common.

For the nonprofit dissolving with liabilities in excess of assets, the Chapter 7 filing is the only route to absolute closure, creating a firewall of protections that most boards will consider prudent and necessary if faced with an insolvent organization. Once the Chapter 7 filing is complete, the board and management hand off total control of the organization to the bankruptcy trustee for the final disposition of assets and final resolution of liabilities. The trustee will follow a prioritization schedule established by the courts to assure a fair distribution of remaining assets.

A major challenge of operating in the Zone of Insolvency is that a period of prolonged financial distress may deplete the funds necessary to pay off all creditors during dissolution. Because dissolution may trigger expenses not on the current balance sheet, the cost of dissolution is easily underestimated. Presumably the nonprofit board will want to manage dissolution so as to avoid bankruptcy if at all possible. It must have a realistic estimate of dissolution costs in mind and manage cash reserves to that number. Once the net assets dip below the dissolution costs, bankruptcy is all but assured.

COSTS OF DISSOLUTION

Most boards have no idea what it would actually cost to close down the nonprofit organization. In fact, the concept of closing costs almost seems counterintuitive; if you close down an organization due to lack of funds, it would seem that the closing would stop the financial hemorrhaging, but that is not always the case in the short term. There are all kinds of costs that may be triggered by the decision to close, and these should be clearly identified prior to the final vote for dissolution.

First, let's consider a fairly simple example of a cost triggered by closure. Assume that a nonprofit organization with 30 staff and an annual budget of $2 million operates an office in leased space. The lease is a five-year lease with 52 months remaining and no termination clause, at a cost of $10,000 per month. The organization has been experiencing financial distress, cash reserves have been depleted, but it is current on all payables. The 52 remaining months on the lease at $10,000 per month represents a tail-end obligation of $520,000. But that obligation does not appear on the balance sheet until the organization files for dissolution. In this case, assuming cash reserves were totally depleted but all payables were current, there would suddenly be a $520,000 liability posted to the balance sheet, with no ability to pay. For the board that had just been watching the balance sheet monthly, the posting of this liability could come as quite a shock.

A good wind-down analysis must include a cash flow projection itemizing all expenses and revenues for the wind-down period and a calculation of final net assets or liabilities. The following list of possible wind-down expenses is typical, but each organization must identify its own winddown expenses based on its specific situation.

Tail-End Obligations on Leased Space

Office leases are often signed at a time of growth, when an organization needs to add space. The optimism that accompanies growth should not overshadow a prudent review of the lease and should envision negotiations for the best terms possible. Negotiating for a reduced monthly rate on the front end in return for a noncancellable, longer, tail-end obligation could be a very bad deal for an organization that subsequently finds itself filing for dissolution. A more prudent approach would be to negotiate for shorter-term leases, even if it requires a higher monthly rate. If the nonprofit organization negotiating the lease is dependent on renewable contracts for revenue, it should make every attempt to coordinate the expiration of the lease with the renewal rate of the contract so that lease obligations do not extend beyond the potential termination date of revenue contracts.

The organization that files for dissolution with tail-end obligations on leases will find that landlords in most states are reluctant to settle for less than the full amount of the obligation. For the organization that cannot pay in full, filing for bankruptcy may be a necessary legal strategy. The bankruptcy trustee has the power to sublease the space or to negotiate with the landlord and scrape away tail-end obligations, especially for leases that were paying less than current market rate for the space.

Tail-End Obligations on Leased Equipment

Office equipment is typically leased in terms of three to five years with no cancellation options. If an organization is going out of business with a tail-end obligation on leased equipment, the leasing company will provide a final close-out figure, which will essentially be a calculation of remaining months on lease plus any appropriate fees. Often leasing companies will not schedule the machine for pickup until the close-out obligation has been paid in full. Ultimately the leasing company is entitled to the full close-out fee and return of the leased property.

Run-off Coverage on Insurance Policies

State law specifies a two- to three-year period of continuing legal liability following the dissolution of any corporation. To deal with this liability, insurance policies such as director's and officer's liability policies or fiduciary liability policies include predetermined rates for run-off policies, which can be purchased in the event of dissolution. The rates are typically defined as a percentage of the most recent annual premium, in the range of 70% per year for the run-off years. These are very important policies to maintain for the protection of the corporation and its board and managers, in the event that there are any legal issues raised during the run-off years related to actions taken prior to the dissolution.

Final Contributions to Employee Pension Plans

Corporate dissolutions for organizations with defined contribution plans are much simpler than for those with defined benefit plans. The defined contribution plans are managed by outside firms; in essence, they are portable funds owned by the individual employees who continue to manage their funds after the dissolution. When evaluating the close-down costs for a corporate dissolution, however, the projections must include all final pension contributions in keeping with corporate policy.

Final Payroll and Employee Benefits

Employee benefits must be included as a real cost in calculating the final close-down costs for a corporation. Legal counsel for dissolution or bankruptcy counsel should be consulted in regard to how to prioritize payment of close-down expenses. Federal bankruptcy laws rank employees as the highest priority in bankruptcy, ahead of tax obligations or general unsecured creditors. Payment, therefore, of final salary, accrued benefits for vacation and sick time (if any), and expense reimbursements for employees should be the highest priority in calculating total close-down expenses.

Attorneys' and Consultants' Fees for Dissolution Filings, Bankruptcy Filings, and Close-Down Management

Legal counsel and consulting help is critical in filing for dissolution and bankruptcy, but attorneys and consultants like to be paid for their work and will be aware of all of the details of the organization's financial status in closing. It is common for close-down counsel and consultants to request a board resolution authorizing the contract for legal services and authorizing a prepaid retainer fee. They will draw down at an hourly rate against the prepaid retainer and return any unused funds to the organization.

Close-Down Accounting and Audits

There is accounting work to be done as part of the close-down, which will require resources after the organization ceases operations. To calculate the total close-down expenses, estimate the cost-handling final resolution of payables and receivables, generating closing financial statements, preparing final year 990s, operations audit, pension audit, pension 550 reports, W2s, and, if the organization received federal funding, a close-out A–133 report. These expenses may include fees for outside auditors and accountants and/or close-down salary for accounting staff.

Liquidation of Property

Liquidation of real property is an essential part of the close-down activity, and again, it comes with a cost. Real estate commissions, auctioneer fees, or fees to "dump and run" or "junk be gone" must be calculated into the total cost of closing.

If the organization will close with net assets, it can reduce close-down expenses by directly managing the liquidation and disposal of real property. If, however, the organization is closing with liabilities greater than assets, great care must be taken. A bankruptcy trustee will prefer to directly manage the liquidation and disposal process to generate maximum revenue for the creditors. If there is any possibility that the organization will file for bankruptcy, it is best to transfer all assets to the trustee for final liquidation. The bankruptcy trustee's concern will be to assure fairness to all creditors and to assure that no party was advantaged to the disadvantage of a creditor in the liquidation process.

Collections of Final Receivables

Once it is known that an organization is going out of business, the payments on receivables will slow considerably. Do not underestimate the degree to which debtors will simply slow pay in hopes that their obligations will be forgotten or overlooked in the close-down process. Aggressively managing receivables during the close-down process is necessary to protect the assets of the corporation and, in the event of bankruptcy, the assets due to the creditors. Failure to manage the receivables at the expense of the creditors can create additional legal liabilities for the corporation.

Payment for Storage of Corporate Records

Every corporation has a legal responsibility to maintain corporate records, many for seven years. Dissolution, in and of itself, does not preclude this requirement. A total calculation of close-down costs should include the expense of storing corporate records as well as payment to an administrator of sorts who will access the records to respond to any legally binding requests for information after closure. In the event of bankruptcy, where there is no money to pay forward on expenses such as records retention, the bankruptcy trustee has the power of the federal courts to dispose of certain corporate records in an effort to eliminate ongoing expenses. Be aware that the corporation has no right to dispose of these records and must comply with all records retention laws and turn the records over, intact, to the bankruptcy trustee, even if the trustee subsequently elects to dispose of them.

Payment for Any Taxes Due

All taxes must be paid as part of dissolution. In the event of bankruptcy, the priorities are typically employees first, taxes second, and then general unsecured creditors. As a practical matter, this means that taxes get paid before general unsecured creditors. Great care must be taken in managing the payables during close-down to assure that the priorities of the bankruptcy court are not inadvertently violated. This is particularly challenging if the organization starts down the road of filing for dissolution by managing the process directly, subsequently realizes that closing liabilities exceed assets, and then files for bankruptcy. In this case, the bankruptcy trustee will scrutinize all financial decisions of the previous two years and may find that the organization somehow failed to protect the interests and rights of the creditors.

Summary of Close-Down Expenses

These close-down expenses are usually incurred after operations cease and, presumably, revenue has slowed to a trickle. A good wind-down plan will minimize expenses by reducing the wind-down period, thereby maximizing final net assets. The cash flow projections for the close-down period must factor remaining receivables and drawdown on cash reserves to project final assets and liabilities.

Board Values When Dissolution Looms

Nonprofit boards typically are not only mission driven but value driven. Typically, the nonprofit board member volunteers to "do good" and help others. Integrity is traditionally a high value for nonprofit organizations and their boards. When dissolution looms, the board is in unfamiliar territory, where the values commitment is challenged in new ways.

Is There an Honorable Way to Dissolve a Nonprofit?

Of course. But here is where feelings and emotions may betray you. The process and decision for dissolution is not likely to feel good. It may be absolutely the right decision, but still it may not feel good at all. Focus on the successes the organization experienced, recognize that nothing lasts forever, and move on. As for honor, there is no perfect formula for closing down an organization, but there should be a way to honor the traditions and reputation of the organization in every aspect of the process.

One board may place a very high premium on assuring that all close-down expenses and tail-end obligations can be paid off by the organization without seeking the protection of bankruptcy. If this is the case, the board is advised to be proactive about closure decisions to assure that enough assets remain to pay the expenses. Another board may place a premium on making every last effort to try to keep the organization alive, but in the process may find itself forced to close with the protection of bankruptcy, because the effort to stay alive has drained the cash reserves to the point that final liabilities exceed remaining assets. Both operated with the best intent.

Is There Inherent Dishonor in Dissolving a Nonprofit?

Not necessarily. If a board finds itself governing a financially distressed nonprofit that is draining its cash reserve and depleting its assets, it can be prudent and honorable to close it down, stop the financial hemorrhaging, and distribute the remaining assets to other nonprofit(s) to further the original intent of the mission. If a board finds that it is governing a nonprofit that has assets but is no longer serving its chartered mission, it may be prudent to close. The average life span of a Fortune 500 company is just 40 years. Nonprofit corporations have no particular right to exist forever.

Consider the Katrina Fund established by Presidents Bill Clinton and George H. W. Bush. Established to raise funds to help rebuild New Orleans and the surrounding area after Hurricane Katrina, it raised several hundred million dollars with a plan to distribute all of the funds and put itself out of business within four years. Great purpose, great success, and dissolution was part of the plan.

What Does It Mean to Dissolve the Nonprofit Organization with Integrity?

Integrity is often discussed when nonprofits consider ceasing operations. Employees who find themselves without jobs may be inclined to question the integrity of the board. Donors who gave sacrificially may be concerned about the financial integrity of how funds were managed. Both board and management must place a premium on truthfulness, but at the same time find that it is not prudent to share all of the business of the organization with all parties. Deceitfulness and even the appearance of deceitfulness must be avoided, at a time when many will not understand the details driving decisions.

Does Filing for Bankruptcy Support or Erode Our Integrity?

There is an aura about bankruptcy that is not pleasant. Most people do not want to be associated with a bankruptcy either personally or as board members of a nonprofit. "Under Roman law, after gathering together and dividing up the assets of a delinquent debtor, the creditors would break the debtor's workbench as a punishment and a warning to other indebted tradesmen. Bankrupt individuals were regarded as thieves who deserved severe penalty."[1]

While filing for bankruptcy is simply a legal process defined by the courts, many assign moral implications. This is not a moral decision, but rather, a legal decision. A board governing a financially distressed organization may at some point find it prudent to consider all legal options, including the filing of bankruptcy. If integrity is the issue, filing for bankruptcy may in fact be the best option the board has to assure fair treatment of all creditors, and failure to file for bankruptcy could erode the creditors' perceptions of board integrity.

If and when a board files for protection of bankruptcy, all of the decisions and actions of that board will be reviewed by the bankruptcy trustee. The trustee will be looking for integrity and compliance with all relevant law. If, prior to the filing, the board took action that advantaged one party of the corporate community while disadvantaging another, the trustee may act to remedy such action.

Must We Avoid Bankruptcy in Order to Preserve Our Integrity, or Is Filing for Bankruptcy the Best Way to Protect Our Integrity?

A board may be proactive in managing its situation so as to be able to avoid the need for bankruptcy in dissolution. But this is not always possible. Another board may find itself, due to events beyond its control, governing an insolvent nonprofit, where filing for bankruptcy is necessary. Neither situation in and of itself guarantees the preservation of integrity.

Is It Ever Appropriate to Dissolve a Solvent Nonprofit with Significant Assets, and If So, What Should the Board Do with the Assets?

Consider the case of a prominent church incorporated in the 1800s and rich in real estate assets. In recent years, the church that once served thousands of members now has just a handful of members. Millions of dollars of real estate are owned debt free, and the operating expenses are more than covered by endowment funds. But the church no longer serves the mission for which it was chartered. The prudent board, having searched in vain for alternative uses, is totally in its rights to file for dissolution. Nonprofit law requires that the bylaws of each nonprofit include a dissolution clause that specifies that remaining assets must be distributed to other nonprofit(s) of similar mission. In this case, the board may liquidate the assets and gift them to another church or ministry, thus furthering the original intent of the organization and its donors. Or the board may arrange for a merger with another church, or gift the property to another church and let that organization handle the liquidation decisions.

FISCAL LIABILITIES OF INDIVIDUAL BOARD MEMBERS

If properly protected by adequate director's and officer's liability insurance, and with the volunteer protection laws of the state of incorporation, nonprofit board members are reasonably protected from personal liabilities for the actions of the board. In fact, the heart of corporate law shifts liabilities from individuals to corporations, a critical component of business transactions and risk analysis. But nonprofit board members are not totally without risk. For example, a nonprofit board member who acts inappropriately with a staff member may face a claim for sexual harassment or sexual misconduct, which is illegal and is specifically excluded from the insurance coverage. But when board members exhibit due diligence and make decisions in accord with the bylaws of the corporation and in keeping with the law, liabilities are minimized.

Great care must be taken by boards governing financially distressed organizations—that is, those operating in the Zone of Insolvency. The bankruptcy courts have taken special interest in recent years in reviewing board decisions made while in the Zone of Insolvency to assure that such decisions were appropriate and did not advantage one party of the corporation while disadvantaging another. The board that takes on new financial obligations while knowing that the organization cannot meet those obligations is not balancing the interests of all parties. If the organization ends up in bankruptcy, the court-appointed trustee may second-guess those decisions and hold the board liable.

DIRECTOR'S AND OFFICER'S LIABILITY INSURANCE DOES NOT PAY OFF DEBT

Corporate insurance should always be carefully evaluated with the assistance of a licensed insurance professional. During a wind-down, insurance needs will change, and they must be closely monitored to minimize expense while assuring adequate protection. State law will define the length of exposure for corporations in dissolution, but often a corporation can be held liable for two years or more after dissolution. During this extended period of liability, the prudent board will want director's and officer's (D&O) liability coverage and fiduciary liability coverage. Most policies include specific options to purchase up to three years of run-off insurance to cover this extended possibility. Costs will typically be 70% of annual premium prior to dissolution, and the insurance must be prepaid.

There is a great deal of misunderstanding about director's and officer's liability insurance. These policies, combined with state laws regarding volunteer protections, provide a level of protection for volunteers serving on nonprofit boards. In the event of a claim, the policy will first pay for legal defense and then pay any resultant awards, up to the maximum defined in the policy. In the event that the final awards exceed the maximum coverage of the policy, the organization and the individual board members could be liable. It is only prudent, therefore, for individuals considering board service to review the D&O insurance coverage, and for all board members to annually review the policy to assure adequate coverage. Many nonprofit boards, in their commitment to frugality, purchase D&O coverage at a level much lower than is adequate.

It is critical for board members to understand their potential exposure corporately and as individuals, and to assure that the D&O coverage is adequate. Second, it is critical that the organization have adequate fiduciary liability insurance to protect against any possible errors or omissions in the management of employee benefits and other fiduciary responsibilities. Last, but not least, it is critical that board members understand that in the event of dissolution, these insurances do not pay off debt. There seems to be a common misperception that somehow these policies would pay for any shortfall in the event that liabilities exceed assets at the time of dissolution, but this is clearly not the case.

Five Great Questions for Your Next Board Meeting

1. What would it cost to close this organization?
2. If we decided today to close this organization, would we complete the close-down with net assets remaining, or net liability?
3. What are the dollar limits in our director's and officer's liability coverage and fiduciary liability coverage, and how do we know the coverage is adequate?
4. If we want to make certain that we could close this organization without filing for bankruptcy, what is the date of no return based on the current burn ratio?
5. Do we have a plan and management in place to minimize risk and expense during the wind-down?

Notes

1. Crown Financial Ministries, "Bankruptcy" pamphlet, www.crown.org/pamphlets/pdfs/bankruptcy.pdf.

CHAPTER 15

Common Characteristics of Financially Distressed Nonprofits

It is my observation, in dealing with many nonprofit organizations of various shapes and sizes, that there are characteristics common to financially distressed nonprofits and other characteristics common to financially strong nonprofits. Not every organization will exhibit all of these characteristics, but in general the categories seem to apply.

INADEQUATE ACCOUNTING SKILLS

I was recently called in to consult with a financially distressed nonprofit that owns and operates a $25 million youth facility. I kept hearing that "the chief financial officer is really a great guy." Curious, I sat down with the financial officer to get a better understanding of the challenges. Innocently, I asked if the organization's accounting system was on a cash basis or accrual basis; I was stunned to learn that the financial officer could not answer and did not even understand the question.

Financially distressed organizations often have insufficient accounting skills at all levels of the organization. Not only must the key accounting staff have adequate training and experience, but staff at all levels should have position-appropriate financial skills. The CEO, for example, need not be a CPA but must be able to read the balance sheet, understand the cash position, understand the difference between fixed and variable expenses, and anticipate issues with receivables. A sales clerk or order processor must have the ability to prepare an invoice, manage financial data entry, and even generate accurate sales reports. Fiscally weak nonprofits are inclined to underinvest not just in skilled accounting staff but in basic position-appropriate financial skills training for the rest of the staff.

Board Not Focused on Financial Metrics

The board sets the tone and direction for the organization, and that includes the organizational dynamics in regard to finances. If the board places a premium on financial accountability, management will follow suit, and the message will trickle down through the staff. If the board is not concerned about financial details, management and staff will not be either. There are a number of board activities that communicate the level of focus on financial matters. The undisciplined board will show just passing interest or less in audits, monthly financial statements, levels of receivables, policies governing donor-restricted gifts, operating ratios, debt, budget, net gains or losses. Organizations that see the important work of the board as mission activity rather than fiduciary duty are doomed to fiscal distress.

Frequent Turnover of Auditors

There was a time when retaining the same auditors consecutively for many years was seen as a good sign of continuity and understanding. But since some of the more public accounting scandals that involved auditors, including case studies in this book, too many consecutive years with the same auditors now gives rise to concerns about complacency and relationships. As a result, changing audit firms every four or five years is now commonplace. But an organization that retains a new audit firm every year generates concerns about the reasons for such frequent change along with the fear that a particular audit firms may not return for a second engagement.

CEO Not Focused on Finances

It is common to hear nonprofit CEOs say that they are not adept at financial management. While identifying professional strengths and weaknesses is good practice, in this case it is essential that the executive then set out on a mission to assure that the financial management of the organization does not suffer. The CEO must learn how to lead the organization, building strong financial policies and systems that assure fiscal integrity and help the organization strengthen its resources for the future. The CEO unskilled in these matters may need to lean more heavily on accountants, auditors, and consultants to build appropriate financial policies, accounting systems, and internal controls. As we saw in the tale of New Era, CEO John Bennett was a disaster with financial details (by his own admission to the judge) and failed to tap into the resources and support of those who could have helped him establish financial policies and systems to protect the integrity of the foundation.

Lack of Accountability

Accountability is generally infectious. When I walk into an organization whose board is serious about its accountability role with the CEO, the culture of accountability will typically trickle down through all levels of the organization. If I walk into an organization where the CEO is not held accountable, or worse yet operates on the assumption of entitlement, that culture of entitlement will trickle down through all levels of the organization. The corporate culture, along with the behavior of leadership and peers, will have tremendous influence on the behavior of all employees. Even the most conscientious employees will take more liberties when immersed in a culture of entitlement.

Too Much Trust, Not Enough Skepticism

This is an area that is particularly difficult for nonprofit organizations and most difficult for faith-based nonprofits. Employees, executives, and even board members are drawn by the nonprofit mission because they want to "do good." Participation is based on feeling good about the mission of the organization. The operating assumption then migrates to an assumption that all other participants have the intent, discipline, and skills to "do good"—that is, operate with integrity at all times. Skepticism is not part of the culture, and it is, in fact, often discouraged. When a board establishes a long-term trust relationship with an executive, it can be difficult to exercise due skepticism, as we saw in the tales of the United Way, AHERF, and the Baptist Foundation of Arizona. In all three cases, the media's skepticism was out ahead of the board's skepticism. With the benefit of time, we can see how the skepticism of the media was initially rejected by boards that defended their trusted executive, only to find in the end that they had been betrayed. One can only wonder how much longer these frauds would have been perpetuated within these organizations had it not been for the skepticism of the media.

Internal Borrowing from Restricted Funds

Nonprofits that are fiscally weak often show a lack of discipline in regard to internal borrowing against restricted funds. When the cash position dips, they succumb to the temptation to transfer funds. This may be a disciplined form of internal borrowing in keeping with board-approved policy. However, it may be a desperate attempt by management to keep the organization afloat and in fact be a violation of board policy or be an action not supported by any board policy. Board policy should reinforce donor intent, thereby protecting donor-restricted funds to ensure that they are never used for a purpose other than that intended by the donor. But not all board-restricted funds are donor-restricted funds, so the policies can vary by the type of fund. In the tale of AHERF, we saw a cash-starved executive team raid hundreds of donor-restricted funds to move over $50 million to operations, thereby violating donor intent and the law.

A particularly onerous and illegal form of borrowing to solve cash flow problems relates to pension funds, employee benefits, employee taxes, and Social Security. It should go without saying that "borrowing" from these funds to float an organization short on cash is certain cause for free room and board in a local prison, but board and management must be diligent in monitoring performance to avoid these violations. Accountability and skepticism are critical.

Lack of Investment Expertise and Policies

Financially weak nonprofits frequently lack investment policies and skills. Many will state wistfully that they wish they had something to invest. Often those that do have something to invest will be inclined to very conservative investments that result in lost opportunity for revenue or in very risky investments in hopes of big gains. Building the institutional discipline and skill to manage investments based on appropriate board policy is new territory for many weaker organizations, but it is critical to success, even if applied to limited funds initially.

Untimely Financial Reporting

Untimely financial reporting is typically explained by vacancies in key accounting positions, system upgrades, and busy cycles of the year. But the board that does not receive timely financial reports is a board at risk.

Management must be held accountable to a reasonable and timely reporting cycle in spite of natural occurrences such as vacancies and system upgrades. Organizations in financial distress will often realize in retrospect that a period of untimely financial reporting masked the true depth of the problem. A board's ability to respond to financial challenges is enhanced by shorter reporting intervals and inhibited by longer gaps in reporting.

Poor Credit

The creditworthiness of an organization and its ability to borrow are key indicators of financial strength that should be monitored aside from any specific intent to borrow. If banks see an organization as a credit risk, the board and management should take note. Inability to borrow or to access a standing line of credit to solve cash fluctuations may handicap an organization and put inordinate pressure on management to solve cash flow problems through unacceptable means, such as internal borrowing of restricted funds in violation of board policy.

Inadequate Board Policies

In the absence of board policies, management and staff will often establish their own operating protocols. If, for example, the board fails to establish policy for reviewing donor-restricted gifts, documenting the restrictions, and monitoring the disbursement of the funds, management will take more liberties with such donations. If the board does not have a policy for reviewing the expense account of the CEO, the CEO is more likely to abuse privileges, as we saw in the tales of the United Way. If the board does not talk regularly about its commitment to avoid conflicts of interest, board members will be inclined to abuse privileges, as we saw with the Baptist Foundation of Arizona. If the board does not have policy regarding budgets, target margins, performance ratios, and risk, management will be inclined to take more risk, as we saw in the tale of the Western Fairfax Christian Ministries.

Too Much Reliance on the Audit

Auditors understand that they are well served by a degree of skepticism about management representations. But donors and boards of nonprofit organizations often have unrealistic expectations about the value of audits.

Certainly an annual audit is a critical component of assuring fiscal integrity, but audits are not guarantees. As we saw in the tales of the Baptist Foundation of Arizona and AHERF, clean audits by internationally recognized audit firms preceded their scandalous collapses. Audits are undeniably valuable, but to place blind trust in the audit is risky business. At best, audits are historical in nature and may not be helpful in identifying sudden changes in the environment that impact future business viability.

Spending Down Cash Reserves

In the tales of the National Alliance of Business and the Electronics Industries Alliance, we saw organizations with net assets manage controlled spend-downs on reserves immediately preceding dissolution while remaining totally solvent. In the tales of AHERF, WICS, and the Baptist Foundation of Arizona, we saw a pattern of drawing down on cash reserves in an effort to reposition the organization for fiscal viability that ultimately ended in bankruptcy. Nonprofits operating in financial distress typically draw down on cash reserves by default, not by design. Often the depletion of assets is masked, at least temporarily, by untimely financial reports or confusing transfers through spin-off corporations.

No Management of Product Life Cycles

Fiscally weak nonprofits rarely if ever assess or attempt to manage product life cycles. Some organizations are single-product (or single-program) entities, and their entire business viability is dependent on one life cycle. Others have multiple products, but fail to anticipate or understand the impact of overlapping life cycles. Failure to understand that an organization's products have matured and are on the decline results in a lack of urgency for new product development. Ultimately, these organizations will fail financially because the revenue drivers run out of steam.

No Environmental Scanning

Fiscally weak nonprofits frequently exhibit a total lack of curiosity about the operating environment. As a result, market changes take them by surprise, and they become more reactive than proactive. One might argue that environmental scanning is too costly for an organization short on cash, but in reality these organizations cannot afford not to scan the environment in hopes of identifying new revenue opportunities.

FIVE GREAT QUESTIONS FOR YOUR NEXT BOARD MEETING

1. In what ways does this organization lock itself into financial distress through its operating systems and policies?
2. What specific actions can we take to move this organization out of perpetual financial distress?
3. Do we have adequate skills in board and management to escape from or avoid the Zone of Insolvency?
4. What is the deductible per claim on our director's and officer's liability insurance, and how would it affect our budget?
5. What are our most significant deficiencies in regard to our financial management?

CHAPTER 16

Common Characteristics of Financially Strong Nonprofits

No discussion about financially strong nonprofit organizations would be complete without mention of Princeton University. The IRS recognizes it as The Trustees for Princeton University, a 501c3 public charity. Others have described it as a major financial institution with a minor educational subsidiary. Interest income from Princeton's $10 billion investment portfolio dwarfs income from tuition, fees, and charitable contributions combined. In fact, if Princeton never collected another dollar of revenue from tuition, fees, or charitable contributions, it would continue to cover all operating expenses and still record annual net gains of several hundred million dollars per year just by living off of the current endowment. In other words, the interest from the endowment can now cover all expenses and at the same time continue to grow the principal out of excess contributions from interest.

Exhibit 16.1 shows that the university had revenues in excess of expenses by $888 million for 2005. In Exhibit 16.2, the impact of the investment income dwarfs income from all other sources. As a result of the enormous endowment, the program ratio is actually on the decrease (percentage of expenditures spent on program expenses) (see Exhibit 16.3), while other income is on the increase (see Exhibit 16.4), and income from program fees such as tuition is a dwindling percentage of total income (see Exhibit 16.5).

Lest you think that financial strength is just for the large nonprofits, look at the great job the American Society of Nuclear Cardiology (ASNC) has done in building financial strength. In 2003, ASNC delivered a net gain of $700,000 on gross revenues of $2.8 million (25%). Beating that

The Trustees for Princeton University

Fiscal Year Ending June 30, 2005

REVENUE	
Contributions	11%
Government Grants	11%
Program Services	14%
Investments	64%
Other	1%
Total Revenue	**$1,888,507,000**

EXPENSES	
Program Services	88%
Administration	10%
Fundraising	2%
Total Expenditures	**$1,003,547,000**

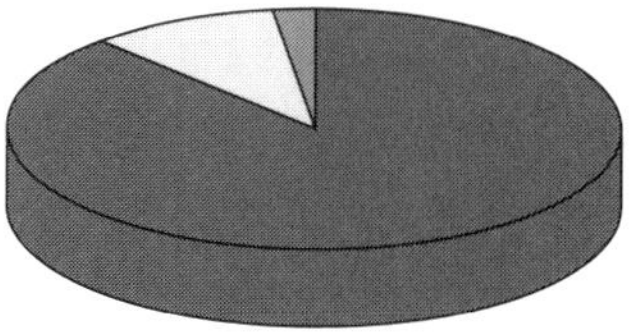

EXHIBIT 16.1 **THE TRUSTEES FOR PRINCETON UNIVERSITY REVENUES AND EXPENSES**

SOURCE: GuideStar, www.guidestar.com.

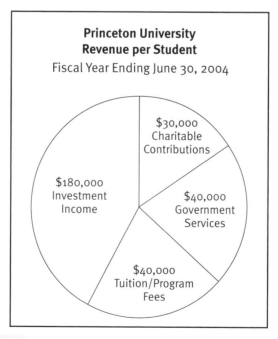

Princeton University Revenue per Student

Fiscal Year Ending June 30, 2004

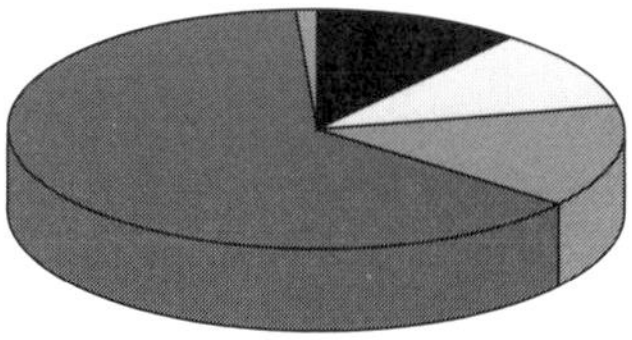

$30,000
Charitable
Contributions
$40,000
Government
Services
$40,000
Tuition/Program
Fees
$180,000
Investment
Income

EXHIBIT 16.2 **PRINCETON UNIVERSITY REVENUE PER STUDENT**

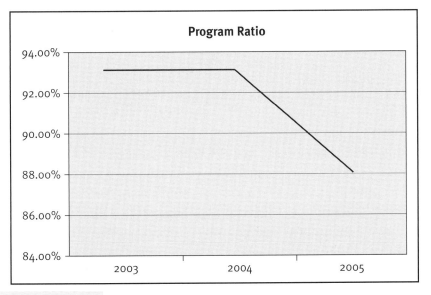

EXHIBIT 16.3   **PROGRAM RATIO**

SOURCE: GuideStar, www.guidestar.com.

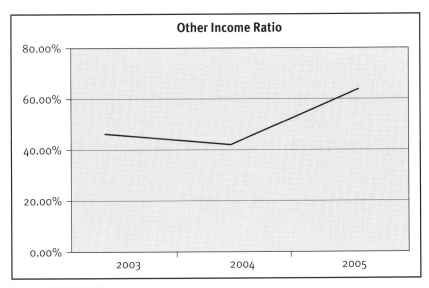

EXHIBIT 16.4   **OTHER INCOME RATIO**

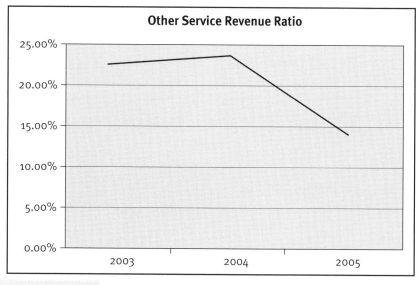

EXHIBIT 16.5   **PROGRAM SERVICE REVENUE RATIO**

SOURCE: GuideStar, www.guidestar.com.

performance in 2004, ASNC delivered a net gain of $987,000 on gross revenue of $3.4 million (see Exhibit 16.6)—and in 2005, a net gain of $585,000 on gross revenue of $3,372,857. The result of this three-year run is a respectable investment portfolio of $4.8 million a nest egg that could carry all of the operating expenses of the organization for 18 months if there were some unforeseen interruption in income. Perhaps the discipline that led to this financial performance is the result of what ASNC learned about the challenges of unforeseen interruptions in income, when its annual convention (and primary source of revenue), scheduled to open in Boston on September 11, 2001, was canceled as a result of the terrorist attacks in New York and Washington, D.C. Regardless of the source of the discipline, ASNC is now nicely positioned for the future, with the ability to fund future growth without hair-raising risk.

There are a number of disciplines that are evident in financially strong nonprofits. No single organization consistently exhibits all of these disciplines, but in my experience with many nonprofits of all sizes and all degrees of financial strength or weakness, financially strong organizations appear to exercise these disciplines more often than financially weak organizations. So which comes first, financial strength or financial discipline? More often than not it is financial discipline that leads to financial

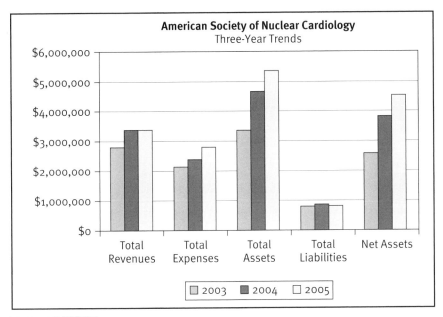

EXHIBIT 16.6   AMERICAN SOCIETY OF NUCLEAR CARDIOLOGY THREE-YEAR TRENDS

SOURCE: GuideStar, www.guidestar.com.

strength. The organization that somehow stumbles into financial strength without financial discipline will find its gains to be short-lived.

RESEARCH AND DEVELOPMENT (R&D) FUNDING

While for-profit corporations understand the critical importance of R&D funding, the nonprofit community as a whole has struggled with this discipline. It is commonplace for nonprofit organizations to have no R&D funding budgeted, with the hope that line managers will somehow squeeze the money out of their operational budgets for new product research and development. This approach typically fails for two key reasons. First, without dedicated R&D funding, the organizational has failed to communicate to staff the critical importance of developing new programs and products. Ironically, nonprofits are often created with an innovative new program or product to launch, but then typically fail to fund future development. Second, without dedicated funding separate from the line manager's operating budget, most line managers will exhibit risk-averse management of budget, protecting the budget for current programs or products but avoiding any risk involved in new product development. Third, without an R&D budget with defined parameters for risk, the organization will not have an acceptable definition of risk. Without the acceptable definition of risk—and an understanding that some new product development projects will inevitably fail—any failure will be perceived as a negative event to be punished rather than understood as part of the cost of new product development.

Nonprofits that have built an R&D funding discipline understand risk and accept losses within certain defined limits. First, a percentage of each annual budget is dedicated to R&D funding. Second, a protocol is announced whereby staff with ideas for new program or product development can apply for project funding. Third, risk is mitigated by diversification; better to risk $1 million by investing in four independent projects costing $250,000 each than to risk it all on one project. If one or two of the projects fail and two or three succeed, the long-term gains exceed the losses, and the losses were not catastrophic but merely a cost of entry.

MANAGING RECEIVABLES

Financially savvy organizations are dead serious about managing receivables. They understand the value of receivables on the balance sheet and are skeptical enough to worry about how real those assets might be. Overly inflated listings of aged or uncollectible receivables can distort the balance sheet, giving a false sense of security. This was the case with the Baptist Foundation of Arizona, where millions of dollars of receivables listed as assets masked the actual insolvent condition of the corporation from auditors, the board, and the public. Organizations that are disciplined about receivables understand the cost of cash float and make every effort to collect receivables in short order, avoiding slow-paying customers and writing off aged and uncollectible accounts.

MANAGING PAYABLES

Every vendor has a perspective on the level of financial savvy of a customer based on the customer's discipline concerning payables. A vendor quickly learns who pays consistently on time and who is slow to pay, or worse. Reasonable businesspeople will take measures to protect themselves against slow-paying organizations by dropping them as clients, charging interest for late pay, raising prices, or periodically refusing to deliver additional product or service until the outstanding balance is paid in full. Financially savvy nonprofits place a premium on consistent and timely payments—a cost-effective way of generating goodwill, attracting quality vendors, and avoiding business interruptions. Some go so far as to negotiate preferred pricing based on payment in advance or payment on delivery.

DONOR-RESTRICTED FUNDS

Any organization of any size can demonstrate bad behavior in regard to the discipline of managing donor-restricted funds, as we learned in the tale of AHERF with Sherif Abdelhak raiding the donor-restricted funds spread throughout his crumbing $2 billion empire. But long-term fiscally strong nonprofits typically have a better discipline in this regard than financially weak organizations. Let's start at the beginning. A donor makes a contribution of funds for a specific designated purpose. The organization can respond in one of three ways: (1) accept the gift and the restrictions, (2) reject the gift, or (3) negotiate with the donor for different terms. Once the gift is accepted with specific designation, the funds are restricted for that purpose.

A reasonable person may assume at this point, that the funds would be set aside in a separate account until disbursed for the designated purpose— a reasonable assumption, but not necessarily a true one. The most disciplined organizations will set these funds aside, so that they are booked as restricted assets, and will not borrow internally against them. In addition, they will govern this discipline with board policy that specifically defines how such funds are to be invested and forbids internal borrowing against them. It is a positive message, assuring the donor of the absolute integrity surrounding use of the funds as designated. Far too many nonprofits have demonstrated lack of discipline in this regard, and they find themselves with restricted funds on the balance sheet as assets that are in reality not funded. As long as the total cash reserves of the organization exceed the total of net restricted assets, they are technically funded, but when the cash reserves drop in a financially distressed organization, the restricted funds line on the balance sheet is suddenly recognized as an unfunded liability.

Board-Restricted Funds

The donor-restricted funds are simply a subset of board-restricted funds. In governing a nonprofit, the board may find it prudent to build institutional discipline around saving for a number of purposes, and board-restricted funds are a helpful tool in this regard. These could be accounts for new product development, purchase of a new building, or simply rainy day cash reserves. Regardless of the purpose, the board-restricted funds are only as good as the board policy governing them and the board's discipline in regard to holding management accountable for implementation of these policies. Again, these policies should specify the intended purpose of the funds, the way they are to be invested, a budget contribution from income, and protocols for draw-downs. Strict adherence to this discipline has been instrumental in building financial strength for many nonprofits.

Cash Flow Management

Financially strong organizations often exhibit totally different discipline surrounding cash flow management than financially weak organizations. Consider the tale of the Western Fairfax Christian Ministries, which, as we saw, ran into significant cash flow problems that threatened its long-term viability and forced huge budget cuts and elimination of over half of the staff positions. Caught up in the euphoria of their growth, they let increased expenses outpace their income as they raised service levels and expanded leased space and staff. Compared with peer organizations, they had minimal net assets to fall back on in the event of any reductions in income and were therefore unable to sustain the ministry at the heightened pace. A strong discipline of cash flow management would have included weekly or even daily monitoring of cash position, projections of cash flow for the upcoming 12 months, and board policy requiring minimum levels of operating cash reserves to even out seasonal fluctuations of income.

Cash flow management is particularly critical for financially distressed organizations that use an accrual basis for accounting. The nonprofit manager who relies on accrual-based financial statements without sufficient attention to cash position will inevitably be blindsided by a cash crisis. Operating with minimal cash reserves, no line of credit, and no ability to borrow, failure to manage cash flow can be catastrophic, leading to inability to meet payroll or worse.

Insurances

Several years ago a Catholic hospital hosted its annual golf outing at a lovely country club. This was a major fundraising event for this particular hospital, complete with a variety of sponsors and contributing partici-pants. As is often the case at golf outings at this level, a local Lincoln dealer agreed to park a brand-new Town Car at one of the par three holes as a hole-in-one prize. Unfortunately, the Sisters organizing the event underestimated the risk and did not understand that insurance should have been purchased to pay for the Town Car in the event of a hole-in-one winner. In fact, they had conducted the event several years in a row without insurance and never had a hole-in-one winner. Unfortunately, on this particular day not one but two participants made the hole-in-one shot, and the hospital had to pay list price for two Town Cars without the benefit of event insurance. This was a hospital that lived with constant financial distress and really needed positive cash flow from the fundraising event.

Financially strong organizations have a different attitude and discipline regarding insurances. This goes beyond just the practical reality of hav-ing more assets to protect. Financially disciplined organizations seem to understand the value and necessity of insurance from the very earliest stages and purchase adequate levels of insurance to protect employees, board, volunteers, and fiscal assets. Less disciplined organizations view insurance as a luxury and typically underestimate the risk and minimize the need for insurance. Director's and officer's liability insurance is one of the policies that financially disciplined organizations scrutinize to ensure adequate coverage. Disciplined organizations are realistic about assessing the level of potential risk and insure accordingly. They also scrutinize the optional levels of policy deductibles and purchase policies that include acceptable levels of potential expense for deductibles. A non-profit with an annual operating budget of $5 million and a D&O policy of $1 million was recently surprised when a claim against the policy triggered a $10,000 deductible, an unanticipated expense that became a real budget hardship for this organization. At the same time, another nonprofit of similar size revealed that its $1 million D&O policy had just a $1,000 deduction per covered event.

In regard to employee coverage, financially savvy organizations will include short-term and long-term disability insurances, whereas distressed organizations often underestimate the risk and cobble together ongoing payments of salary during periods of disability or leave the disabled employee without income. Given the modest salaries typically paid by distressed organizations, the lack of disability coverage adds a very real financial burden to employees suffering disability, or, if the organization tries to pay salary during disability, creates a financial hardship for the organization.

Own Real Estate Rather Than Lease

Numerous fiscally strong nonprofits have built that strength on the foundation of real estate sufficient for all or most for their operational needs. The organizations that were disciplined enough in the early years to build reserves for the purchase of real estate and then managed the cash flow necessary to continue to own and maintain that real estate have typically built significant net asset value. With that net asset value, these organizations now have the ability to borrow against that asset or obtain a line of credit to manage cash fluctuations.

Performance-Based Compensation

In general, nonprofits have not demonstrated adequate sophistication in regard to managing compensation based on performance. Driven by the bottom line and the absolute requirement to deliver a return on investment, for-profit corporations have aggressively honed performance-based compensation skills, experimenting with various arrangements. But the mission-driven purpose of the nonprofit organization often overshadows any requirement for bottom-line performance or return on investment. As a by-product of being soft on bottom-line performance, nonprofits are typically not very disciplined about performance-based compensation.

Some go so far as to argue that performance-based payments are antithetical to the mission of the organization.

Ironically, performance-based compensation offers an opportunity to ensure that organizations are getting a return on their investment in employees, and this would logically be a high priority for nonprofit organizations anxious to demonstrate their cost-effective value to donors and members. Nonprofits with significant fee-for-service revenue have the greatest opportunity for measuring performance and compensation based on those metrics. Stock held for-profit organizations have an inherent opportunity to issue key employees stock, thereby assuring that if they add value for the corporation (i.e., raise stock values), they will be compensated proportionately. Without stocks, nonprofits find it more challenging to develop adequate compensation incentives to challenge performance.

The tale of AHERF is an interesting and important study in performance-based compensation issues for nonprofits. Arguably, the extraordinary number of highly paid executives was a poor investment since the organization ultimately failed and filed for bankruptcy. A successful performance-based program would have assured that compensation was paid based on desired deliverables, which would presumably have included solvency. What is important here is that high salaries do not necessarily equate to performance-based compensation. As a practical matter, nonprofits frequently compensate primarily through salaries, with minimal use of bonuses and commissions, and no opportunity to compensate through stock options. As a result, highly compensated employees are more likely to be paid through salaries in the nonprofit arena, and through a mix of salaries, bonuses, commissions, and stock issues in the for-profit organization.

SKILLS-BASED HIRING

Financially strong nonprofits are more disciplined about skills-based hiring than their weaker counterparts. On the surface, all would pay lip service to skills-based hiring, but many miss the mark, hiring based on personality, personal preferences, connections, or politics. The lack of discipline exhibited by many in this regard actually weakens the performance of the organization and results in compensation expense with poor return on investment. This problem becomes part of the organizational culture, making it difficult for any one department or hiring manager to break through to skills-based hiring. And if hired, the highly skilled employee will represent a threat to less-skilled hires and face formidable opposition from entrenched but underskilled employees.

COMPETITIVE COMPENSATION

Financially strong nonprofits are more likely than their weaker cohorts to establish competitive compensation based on local market rates. Failure to set competitive rates leaves organizations with lower-performing hires and longer position vacancy rates. Savvy organizations use the competitive pay rates to draw the most experienced and well-trained staff, enhance employee retention, and reduce the length of position vacancies between hires.

BUDGET DISCIPLINE

Fiscally strong nonprofits are more likely to be disciplined about budget management, meeting or beating budget goals regularly. Weaker organizations place less priority on budget discipline, repeatedly performing worse than budget. Each organization has its own unique culture, and budget discipline—or lack thereof—seems to permeate organizations from top to bottom. Rare is the manager who will demonstrate budget discipline when surrounded by managers who place no value on such discipline.

CONTRACT MANAGEMENT POLICY

Regardless of size, it is the financially strong organizations that build a management discipline in regard to contracts. This begins with board policy that assigns contract-signing authority to management with specific limitations, and follows down through various levels of management with administrative protocols. These protocols should define multiple bid requirements, legal review, business review, and signature authorities at defined expense levels. On the back end, the policy should specify requirements for records retention, payment authorizations, and long-term operational responsibility.

Brand Management Policy

Organizations that exhibit fiscal strength and discipline are also more likely to exhibit discipline in regard to brand management. The corporate culture respects the value of the brand as well as the need to be intentional about branding. This is not to suggest that all fiscally strong nonprofits have good brand-management disciplines, but rather to suggest that good brand-management skills are more likely to exist in organizations that also demonstrate fiscal discipline. Over time, brand-management discipline brings value to the organization that builds financial strength.

Policy Governance

For the most part, fiscally strong nonprofits are more inclined to policy governance, and weaker organizations are more inclined to administrative boards. Organizations that are performing at an acceptable level of fiscal strength and policy governance may find that the onset of financial distress brings with it a great temptation for the board to move from policy governance back to hands-on administration in an effort to remedy the situation. The board that works through this temptation and maintains its commitment to policy governance will solve the financial distress at an entirely different level than the board that yields to the temptation of stepping back into administrative functions.

Pricing for Profitability

Fiscally disciplined organizations are, in general, more disciplined about pricing strategies. Weaker nonprofits often practice pricing by default, failing to analyze sales patterns or test price effectiveness. This results in underpricing or, worse yet, loss of sales due to price resistance. Pricing by committees or by executive fiat rarely results in revenue maximization for any organization.

Annual Net Gains

Fiscally strong nonprofits are strongly focused on delivering net gains every year. It is part of the culture expected by the board, and employees at all levels are trained to understand the value of net gains and to deliver them annually. They see no moral or ethical conflict in the practice of generating net gains for the nonprofit to provide for future expansion of the mission. Weaker organizations do not exhibit the same resolve and sometimes engage in internal debate, with some staff arguing that a nonprofit has no right to generate net gains.

NEW PRODUCT DEVELOPMENT

Financially strong nonprofits understand that products and programs have life cycles that include periods of infancy, growth, maturity, and obsolescence. They track and project the life cycle stages of each product and work aggressively to introduce new products at appropriate intervals to offset revenue decreases from aging products. They know when to anticipate continued growth and when to terminate an aging product. Exhibit 16.7 demonstrates a fairly balanced life cycle projection for a series of products. As one product begins to decline, another product is growing, thereby offsetting any losses in revenue. In this example, the organization is not growing, but maintains a fairly even net from products. Note that the larger the valley between the various products on the chart, the greater the fluctuations in net revenue. And growth demands even tighter management of product life cycles, with increases in the combined size of products in the growth mode.

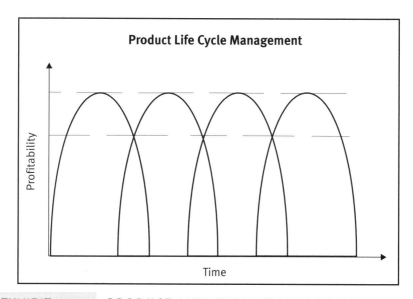

EXHIBIT 16.7   PRODUCT LIFE CYCLE MANAGEMENT

Management Dashboards

Financially strong nonprofits are more likely than their weaker cohorts to effectively use a management dashboard featuring critical performance benchmarks. These dashboards, typically delivered as single-page snapshots featuring 12 to 15 critical metrics, are actively used by the board and the management team in status reports.

Five Great Questions for Your Next Board Meeting

1. Does this organization consistently exhibit behaviors that lead to financial strength?
2. What practices of this organization limit its ability to build financial strength?
3. Do we understand the status and implications of our product life cycles?
4. Is this organization adequately insured for its true risk?
5. In what ways are we actively assessing and managing this organization's risks?

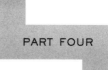

PART FOUR

The Cure

CHAPTER 17

Assessment

A ssessment is a critical first step toward a cure. This chapter features a 20-point assessment of your nonprofit organization that will position you for action. For each of the 20 points, you will assign one of three ratings identifying your organization. By totaling the columns, you will have a sense of the dominant rating for your organization.

Leader of the Pack is the rating for organizations best positioned for financial success and ongoing solvency, standing head and shoulders above peer organizations. Any size organization can achieve this rating, but relatively few do.

Addicted to Mediocrity is the rating for static organizations stuck in the status quo and in need of change. These organizations have accepted complacency and are not engaged in the tenacious pursuit of greater performance. They are usually solvent but drift in and out of the Zone of Insolvency.

Chasing Windmills is the rating for unfocused activity that is unlikely to be productive even when successful, and most likely to mire you in financial distress. These are organizations that are perpetually in the Zone of Insolvency and falling through the zone toward total insolvency.

Take the time to work through these 20 points and rate your organization. Indicate your ratings by line item in the summary chart on the following page, and total each column.

SOLVENCY

Leader of the Pack

You are Leader of the Pack if your organization has always been strongly in the solvency column, never in the Zone of Insolvency, never insolvent. This does not mean that the organization has never experienced any financial

Assessment	Leader of the Pack	Addicted to Mediocrity	Chasing Windmills
Solvency			
Net Assets			
Product Life Cycles			
Business Viability			
Debt			
Receivables			
Payables			
Tail-End Obligations			
Unfunded Depreciation			
Pricing			
Fixed Overhead			
Fundraising			
Compensation Strategy			
Liquidity			
Cash Management			
Peer Group Comparisons			
Uninsured Risk			
Information Technology			
Governance			
Human Resources			
Totals			

stress. Stress is relative, and what stresses one person or organization does not necessarily stress another. Leaders of the Pack keep themselves squarely in the solvency column by responding to financial pressures and making adjustments rather than floating into the Zone of Insolvency.

Addicted to Mediocrity

You are Addicted to Mediocrity if your organization has lived on the line, predominantly solvent but drifting in and out of the Zone of Insolvency. Some organizations dwell in the Zone of Insolvency from their founding forward. Others drift into the Zone of Insolvency at some point in time and never find their way out. In any event, the organization that has been living in the Zone of Insolvency has grown numb, insensitive to the risk that keeps it in perpetual financial distress, and accepts that as a normal state of affairs.

Chasing Windmills

You are Chasing Windmills if your organization is in the insolvency column or has been moving through the Zone of Insolvency toward the insolvency column. Many assume that once a nonprofit is insolvent, it immediately goes out of business, but this is not necessarily the case. The board must constantly assess the condition of the nonprofit and take appropriate action. Drifting through the Zone of Insolvency toward or into the insolvency column should send off warning signals in the minds of board and management. This trend, left uncorrected, is a sure indicator of ultimate failure.

Net Assets

Leader of the Pack

You are Leader of the Pack if your organization's net assets are equal to more than six months' equivalent of the annual operating expenses and continuing to increase. This general rule of thumb may vary depending on the sector. A facility-intensive organization such as a university or hospital will have a much higher net asset ratio than a simple social services agency with minimal facility requirements. Peer group comparisons are the best way to fine-tune this benchmark.

Addicted to Mediocrity

You are Addicted to Mediocrity if your organization's net assets are three to six months' equivalent of the annual operating expenses and have not been increasing. Failure to build net assets will ultimately weaken the fiscal strength and sustainability of the nonprofit. The organization focused on financial survival loses sight of the need to build net assets.

Chasing Windmills

You are Chasing Windmills if your organization's net assets are less than the equivalent of three months' operating expenses and are decreasing. Choosing to spend down the accumulated assets may appear to be a short-term solution, but it typically brings on long-term challenges. Worse yet is the unmanaged, unintended, and unrealized depletion of net assets.

PRODUCT LIFE CYCLES

Leader of the Pack

You are Leader of the Pack if you are actively managing product life cycles and your top three revenue products have offsetting growth and demise curves that minimize the cash flow valleys. Leaders understand that no product lasts forever; they are diligent about new product development and implementation timed to reduce the risks of potential revenue loss associated with mature products at the tail end of their product life cycles.

Addicted to Mediocrity

You are Addicted to Mediocrity if you are not actively managing product life cycles but are fortunate enough that you have not experienced significant revenue variations as a result of maturing products. Without more attention to product life cycle management, your organization will eventually be caught by surprise fluctuations in revenue based on the life cycle ups and downs of key products.

Chasing Windmills

You are Chasing Windmills if you have not been actively managing product life cycles and if, on inspection, you find that your top three revenue products have identical life cycles and will all mature simultaneously. This worst possible scenario has three top revenue products all having reached peak maturity and free falling simultaneously down the back side of the productive life cycle, resulting in severe drops in revenue with little or no offsetting new product revenue.

BUSINESS VIABILITY

Leader of the Pack

You are Leader of the Pack if your organization is conducting ongoing environmental scans, understands its position in a changing market, and shows indications of sustainable income with net operating margins. With attention to environmental changes, most organizations can identify risks as well as new opportunities and can initiate strategic moves to reposition the organization to move successfully into the future.

Addicted to Mediocrity

You are Addicted to Mediocrity if your organization does not conduct environmental scans and cannot articulate its position in the market. In essence, this is an organization with its head in the sand, hoping that the world will not change. Failing to understand changing market conditions will lead to failed products and programs and jeopardize the long-term viability of the organization.

Chasing Windmills

You are Chasing Windmills if your organization does not conduct environmental scanning, cannot articulate its position in the market, has minimal cash reserves, has a history of flat or decreasing revenue, and has a history of not generating annual net gains. This is a spiral that is exceptionally difficult to escape, because escape requires new resources at a time when funding any activity is increasingly difficult.

DEBT

Leader of the Pack

You are Leader of the Pack if your organization carries no debt. Larger organizations with significant facilities requirements may be leaders in this category by managing debt ratios to levels significantly better than peer organizations. In either event, leaders in this category are not overwhelming their budgets with unreasonable expenses for debt service.

Addicted to Mediocrity

You are Addicted to Mediocrity if your organization has debt equal to or greater than your annual expenses. Complacency about debt and the drain of debt service will weaken the fiscal strength of the organization over the long term. Debt is not always inappropriate, but complacency about debt levels can mire an organization in a swamp without much hope of escape.

Chasing Windmills

You are Chasing Windmills if your organization has increasing debt levels in excess of annual operating expenses and debt service expense significantly exceeds that of peer organizations. Ability to emerge from underneath the burden of debt will be further impeded by lack of net assets.

RECEIVABLES

Leader of the Pack

You are Leader of the Pack if your organization's receivables equal less than 10% of your annual expense budget and at least 95% are less than 60 days aged. This must also be evaluated in regard to the collectibility of the remaining receivables. Poor-quality or risky collectibles must be factored into the equation.

Addicted to Mediocrity

You are Addicted to Mediocrity if your organization's receivables are in the range of 10% to 20% of your annual expenses and 5% to 10% are aged 60 days or older. This may be adjusted if the remaining receivables are at high risk of not being recovered. Inadequate collections policies and procedures are a likely factor.

Chasing Windmills

You are Chasing Windmills if your organization's receivables are equal to more than 20% of your annual expenses and more than 20% are aged more than 60 days. This must be viewed in light of the quality of the receivables, which may indicate additional risk for doubtful collection. Organizations weak in this area typically are not monitoring or managing collections in a structured way, and management is not being held accountable by the board.

PAYABLES

Leader of the Pack

You are Leader of the Pack if your organization is always current on payables. This discipline is a competitive advantage enabling organizations to secure better-quality service contracts at lower negotiated cost.

Addicted to Mediocrity

You are Addicted to Mediocrity if your organization often runs 30 to 60 days late on payables. This condition creates a competitive disadvantage, with contractors and creditors not as willing to negotiate favorable terms.

Chasing Windmills

You are Chasing Windmills if your organization runs more than 60 days late on payables. This is a trap that is particularly difficult to escape as it requires simultaneously paying back and paying forward. Ultimately the organization will find it difficult to secure vendors or will pay a higher rate for contract services due to its reputation for slow pay.

TAIL-END OBLIGATIONS

Leader of the Pack

You are Leader of the Pack if your organization could close today and pay off all tail-end obligations, including real estate leases, equipment leases, loans, accounting, and legal expenses, and still have net assets remaining.

Addicted to Mediocrity

You are Addicted to Mediocrity if your organization has tail-end obligations that would be due and payable in the event of closure equal to your net assets, or if the organization does not regularly monitor such obligations.

Chasing Windmills

You are Chasing Windmills if your organization has tail-end obligations and wind-down expenses that would be due and payable in the event of closure in excess of your net assets. This makes an organization particularly vulnerable to cash flow fluctuations, which could ultimately force dissolution or even bankruptcy filing.

UNFUNDED DEPRECIATION

Leader of the Pack

You are Leader of the Pack if your organization books and funds all depreciation. This assures that funds will be available to replace depreciated assets when necessary. Leaders of the Pack do not experience a cash flow crisis or launch another fundraising appeal every time a depreciated asset needs to be replaced.

Addicted to Mediocrity

You are Addicted to Mediocrity if your organization books but does not fund depreciation. This creates a more realistic balance sheet but leaves the challenge of replacing depreciated assets out of debt or current income or fundraising appeals.

Chasing Windmills

You are Chasing Windmills if your organization is not even booking depreciation. Your balance sheets are not a realistic picture of your true financial position. The balance sheets are understating organizational liabilities that exist in reality even though they are not recorded on the balance sheet. If and when you are forced to borrow to pay for replacement of depreciated assets, the debt will appear on the balance sheet, but the liability has actually existed all along. Your donors are most likely fatigued by your never-ending stream of appeals for funds to replace depreciated assets.

PRICING

Leader of the Pack

You are Leader of the Pack if your organization has a strategic pricing strategy that maximizes contribution to margin and supports long-term fiscal strength. Leaders of the Pack understand the difference between fixed and variable costs and use that knowledge strategically in pricing and business planning.

Addicted to Mediocrity

You are Addicted to Mediocrity if you are pricing by default and not managing contribution to margin within designated ranges. This is a common state for many nonprofits, often pricing by committee or by whims of individual managers, without a full understanding of fixed and variable expenses or of the impact of volume on net.

Chasing Windmills

You are Chasing Windmills if your organization's lack of pricing strategy results in products that generate no contribution to margin, subsidized by others that generate significant contributions to margin. Ultimately the market will reject overpriced products that are used to subsidize losers.

Fixed Overhead

Leader of the Pack

You are Leader of the Pack if your organization manages fixed overhead to meet established benchmarks based on best-in-class peer organizations. Leaders of the Pack recognize the danger of locking into excessive fixed overhead and monitor these ratios diligently.

Addicted to Mediocrity

You are Addicted to Mediocrity if your organization has not analyzed fixed overhead ratios or established benchmarks based on best-in-class peer organizations. These organizations are vulnerable to drifting into fixed overhead commitments that are not sustainable.

Chasing Windmills

You are Chasing Windmills if your organization's fixed overheads are increasing, are not managed to any particular benchmark, and exceed best-in-class peer organizations. Fluctuations in volume will create financial crisis and jeopardize the long-term viability of the organization.

FUNDRAISING

Leader of the Pack

You are Leader of the Pack if your organization's fundraising expenses are less than those of peer organizations and generate more funds than peer organizations. These organizations understand that fundraising is a long-term commitment and invest accordingly.

Addicted to Mediocrity

You are Addicted to Mediocrity if your organization does not have a record of sustainable and increasing contribution income. Organizations that are repeatedly hiring and firing fundraisers without building an ongoing sustainable and systematic fundraising function are Addicted to Mediocrity.

Chasing Windmills

You are Chasing Windmills if your organization's fundraising activities are fragmented, fluctuate wildly from year to year, or have high expense ratios compared with peer organizations. These organizations fail to build sustainable systems for fundraising and are therefore always scrambling to catch up. High staff turnover is typical, and all fundraising failures are blamed on the staff.

COMPENSATION STRATEGY

Leader of the Pack

You are Leader of the Pack if your organization has a compensation strategy that pegs compensation to specific local market benchmarks that enable you to hire quality staff. This does not necessarily mean paying at the highest scale, but rather paying at a scale that will create a competitive advantage in hiring and retention.

Addicted to Mediocrity

You are Addicted to Mediocrity if your organization is constantly disadvantaged when trying to hire and retain competent staff because of insufficient compensation. These organizations are forced to hire staff that are less than optimal, and may actually spend more dollars overall on staffing by hiring extra staff to compensate for skills deficiencies.

Chasing Windmills

You are Chasing Windmills if your organization is forced to hire inexperienced and unskilled staff due to inferior compensation and you do not have a compensation strategy.

LIQUIDITY

Leader of the Pack

You are Leader of the Pack if you have operating cash reserves more than sufficient to manage typical month-to-month fluctuations in cash flow without external borrowing. These organizations have board policies establishing reserve fund levels and defining approved uses and repayment terms for internal borrowing from reserve funds.

Addicted to Mediocrity

You are Addicted to Mediocrity if you are using commercial lines of credit to solve month-to-month fluctuations in cash flow. These organizations will pay off the debt at least once annually, only to borrow again to meet the cash demands of the next seasonal shortage.

Chasing Windmills

You are Chasing Windmills if you do not have an operational cash reserve to handle month-to-month fluctuations in cash flow and if you cannot obtain a sufficient line of credit to solve these same cash flow fluctuations. Such organizations often delay payables to solve cash flow problems or miss payroll deadlines.

CASH MANAGEMENT

Leader of the Pack

You are Leader of the Pack if your organization has regular cash flow reports, projections of cash flow by month for the budget year, and operating cash reserves to cover all monthly fluctuations without commercial borrowing. Management keeps the board appraised of cash positions, projects cash flow needs, and manages cash demands by internal borrowing against operational cash reserves.

Addicted to Mediocrity

You are Addicted to Mediocrity if your organization is projecting cash flow fluctuations, anticipating shortfalls, and borrowing commercially to meet seasonal shortfalls.

Chasing Windmills

You are Chasing Windmills if your organization has no cash flow projection reports and is constantly reacting to cash shortages by scrambling for cash, delaying payables, engaging in unauthorized internal borrowing, or missing payroll deadlines.

Peer Group Comparisons

Leader of the Pack

You are Leader of the Pack if your organization has established strategic benchmarks with input from board and management, comparing performance with peer groups and best-in-class organizations.

Addicted to Mediocrity

You are Addicted to Mediocrity if your organization has not established strategic benchmarks and is not aware of peer group performance.

Chasing Windmills

You are Chasing Windmills if your organization is significantly below peer groups in standardized performance measures.

Uninsured Risk

Leader of the Pack

You are Leader of the Pack if your organization has a structured risk management function and is appropriately insured for risk.

Addicted to Mediocrity

You are Addicted to Mediocrity if your organization has basic insurances without in-depth risk analysis or a structured risk management function. These organizations will proudly state that they are insured, without realizing that they are significantly underinsured given the true level of risk.

Chasing Windmills

You are Chasing Windmills if your organization has never conducted a comprehensive risk management analysis, has no risk management function, and is underinsured for risk.

INFORMATION TECHNOLOGY

Leader of the Pack

You are Leader of the Pack if your organization maintains information technology systems with adequate hardware, current versions of software, fully developed management reports, and sufficient staff training on use of systems.

Addicted to Mediocrity

You are Addicted to Mediocrity if your organization is using outdated or insufficient hardware, is running several versions behind on software upgrades, has not developed adequate management reports, and has marginal staff training on use of systems.

Chasing Windmills

You are Chasing Windmills if your information technology is an eclectic collection of software applications rather than an integrated system, forcing time-consuming and labor-intensive double entry and failing to provide timely management reports needed for staff to manage their functional responsibilities.

GOVERNANCE

Leader of the Pack

You are Leader of the Pack if your organization maintains a quality board committed to policy governance and accountability.

Addicted to Mediocrity

You are Addicted to Mediocrity if your board defers to the CEO and drifts from policy governance to administration and back again. These organizations typically experience challenges in maintaining skilled executives because of the muddy lines of accountability.

Chasing Windmills

You are Chasing Windmills if your board engages primarily in administrative tasks and does not maintain an ongoing policy book.

HUMAN RESOURCES

Leader of the Pack

You are Leader of the Pack if your organization is committed to skills-based hiring, utilizes pre-employment skills and aptitude testing of candidates, and successfully retains skills-competent staff. The commitment to skills-based hiring prevails over "insider" hiring connections.

Addicted to Mediocrity

You are Addicted to Mediocrity if your organization subscribes to skills-based hiring but does not engage in pre-employment skills and aptitude testing of candidates.

Chasing Windmills

You are Chasing Windmills if your organization selects staff based on relationships rather than skills competencies, does not discuss the issue, and does not utilize any pre-employment candidate skills testing.

WHAT IS YOUR ASSESSMENT?

If your assessment indicates that your predominant rating is Leader of the Pack, congratulations. You are ranked with a small group of high-performing peers in the nonprofit community. Take pride in this achievement, but remember *Jurassic Park;* the dinosaurs will escape from the reserve and the natural state of organizations is chaos. Now is the time to act on your strengths with an action plan to ensure that you will continue to avoid the Zone of Insolvency.

If your assessment indicates that your organization is Addicted to Mediocrity, roll up your sleeves and get to work bolstering the weakest line items and reinforcing your strengths. Your organization has some challenges, but it has survived this long and has a foundation on which to build. Recognize that the world has changed and that the risks of continuing in financial distress are higher than ever. Commit to building financial strength that will secure your mission well into the future. If your organization is on a downward drift through the Zone of Insolvency and you conclude that it is not viable in the future, arrange a merger or consider dissolution.

If your assessment indicates that your predominant rating is Chasing Windmills, it is time to make some tough decisions. In light of the risks of the current reality, consider the pros and cons of your three options: (1) a fix, (2) a merger, or (3) dissolution. By rating predominantly in this category, it appears that fixing the organization will be an extraordinary challenge. If you are determined to continue, a merger may be the best option. If you determine that the organization is not fixable, dissolution may be most appropriate outcome.

FIVE GREAT QUESTIONS FOR YOUR NEXT BOARD MEETING

1. What does our assessment tell us about of our current organizational strengths?
2. What does our assessment tell us about our current organizational weaknesses?
3. Do we as a board see the CEO as part of the problem or part of the solution?
4. Are we as a board part of the problem or part of the solution?
5. What does our assessment tell us about the priorities for this board over the next two years?

CHAPTER 18

Acknowledgment

Change begins with acknowledging a problem. The nonprofit board and management team that cannot conduct an assessment and then acknowledge the true nature of the situation will not change. This kind of acknowledgment can be tough, but it frees the organization up to commit to action. Those who have dealt with personal addictions know the power and absolute necessity of looking into the mirror and acknowledging a problem. Acknowledgment is difficult for an individual and even more difficult for boards. To sit around a board table with a group of respected peers and acknowledge that "we have a problem" is not comfortable, but without acknowledgment the organization cannot move to solutions.

WE ARE IN THE ZONE OF INSOLVENCY

Now that the assessment is complete, it is time to build consensus around the board table. Perhaps, based on the assessment, it is time to acknowledge that "we have been operating in the Zone of Insolvency." Uncomfortable words. Powerful words. Words that set the stage for a commitment to action. Some boards will arrive quickly at a consensus statement. Others will struggle to find consensus. For some organizations, it will be the management team that lands first and encourages the board acknowledgment. For others, it may be a small number of board members, or an individual board member who first voices the acknowledgment. Whatever the case, the discussion demands attention and the utmost respect for diverse opinions. It is a discussion that requires resolution, one that cannot be tabled.

WE ALONE ARE RESPONSIBLE FOR OUR CURRENT STATE OF AFFAIRS

Part of the acknowledgment is to accept responsibility for the current state of affairs. "We are in the Zone of Insolvency, and we alone are responsible." Acknowledging that the management team, and ultimately the board, has responsibility focuses the discussion. Excuses are myriad, but they muddy the waters when it comes to committing to action. Yes, the fundraising efforts have not proven sustainable, but ultimately it is the responsibility of the board and management team to find alternatives. Yes, the market has changed, but it is the responsibility of the board and management team to position the organization for effective service, arrange for a merger, or file for dissolution. Yes, the organization was victimized by a bizarre Ponzi scheme that duped thousands, but it is the responsibility of the board and management team to demonstrate a prudent level of skepticism in order to protect the assets of the corporation. Yes, an unscrupulous employee raided the organization's bank account, but it is the responsibility of the board to establish policies and monitor performance to protect against such behavior.

OUR ACTIONS AND POLICIES HAVE LANDED US IN THIS STATE OF AFFAIRS

"We are in the Zone of Insolvency, and we alone are responsible. It is our actions and policies that landed us in this state of affairs." The acknowledgment needs to deal with specific actions and policies (or lack thereof) that contributed to the problem. For those dealing with a weight-control problem, identifying the trigger foods that contribute to overeating is a critical part of the acknowledgment that frees the individual to commit to action that will result in the desired outcome. Likewise, the nonprofit board and management team must identify the specific triggers that lock the organization into perpetual financial distress.

Some organizations speak openly about specific past decisions that created financial distress and turned out to be ill advised. Others bury such memories, feeling they are too painful to discuss. For some organizations, it is not policies or actions that need to be acknowledged but rather the lack of action or lack of policies that contributed to the current state of affairs.

Develop a list of specifics that have contributed to your organization's problems as part of the acknowledgment process.

Our Organizational Culture Plays a Role in Our Current State of Affairs

"We are in the Zone of Insolvency, and we alone are responsible. It is our actions and policies that have landed us in this state of affairs. Our organizational culture plays a role in our current state of affairs." Acknowledge the role of the culture and accept that the board and management team are responsible for establishing the tone and value system of the culture. An organization that has developed a culture of entitlement will inevitably experience employees at all levels taking liberties with the assets of the corporation. An organization that has a culture of frugality may find it difficult to invest in new product development and future growth. Rebuilding financial integrity and discipline in a culture of entitlement will be difficult if not impossible.

We Have the Ability to Change Our Culture and Our Behavior

"We are in the Zone of Insolvency, and we alone are responsible. It is our actions and policies that have landed us in this state of affairs. Our organizational culture plays a role in our current state of affairs. We have the ability to change our culture and our behavior." The acknowledgment is not just a litany of negatives. Acknowledging the ability to change is a very positive aspect, offering light and hope. Without hope, the acknowledgment process will be bogged down in a gloomy pit of despair.

We Have the Responsibility to Change

"We are in the Zone of Insolvency, and we alone are responsible. It is our actions and policies that have landed us in this state of affairs. Our organizational culture plays a role in our current state of affairs. We have the ability and responsibility to change our culture and our behavior." The acknowledgment is complete. It recognizes the current state of affairs and establishes responsibility. It recognizes the role of the organizational culture as an environmental issue that may need to be changed. And looking forward, it recognizes the ability and responsibility to change.

This may be the shortest chapter in the book, but the acknowledgment process is absolutely critical in committing to change. If the board and management team are not serious about their acknowledgment of the current state of affairs, they will, at best, make only tepid commitments to action. When the action steps are difficult to implement, the organization that has not seriously acknowledged the current status will flounder and second-guess itself. It is the sound acknowledgment of the problem, with strong consensus, that builds the foundation on which commitment and action can succeed.

FIVE GREAT QUESTIONS FOR YOUR NEXT BOARD MEETING

1. What role have we as a board played in regard to the current financial status of the organization?
2. Do we as a board believe that we can choose to escape from or avoid the Zone of Insolvency?
3. To what degree have we as a board blamed our problems on management?
4. Is there a specific area of responsibility that we as a board have been neglecting?
5. Do we really believe that we have ultimate responsibility for the future of the organization?

CHAPTER 19

Commitment

In the first 18 chapters, we have reviewed 10 case studies of nonprofit organizations of different shapes and sizes from a variety of sectors, following their paths through solvency, the Zone of Insolvency, and actual insolvency. We have seen that there are many paths and many variables along those paths that contribute to the outcomes of solvency, the Zone of Insolvency, or total insolvency. The well-intentioned efforts of boards and executives with impeccable integrity can result in success, but sometimes in failure. Financial distress can follow unskilled management, nefarious or illegal deeds of staff or board, or simply changes in market conditions. We defined the Zone of Insolvency as a zone of financial distress where reasonable people might at least foresee the possibility of insolvency, and we identified the legally expanded role of boards in governing organizations in the Zone of Insolvency. We learned that since the courts identified expanded responsibilities for boards governing in the Zone of Insolvency (1992), and since regulators have focused increasingly on holding boards accountable for their actions (Sarbanes Oxley, Nonprofit Integrity Act of California), there are ever-increasing liabilities associated with serving on a corporate (nonprofit) board. In Chapter 17 we offered a structured approach to assessing the current state of your nonprofit organization, and in Chapter 18 we established the need for board and management to acknowledge the current state of affairs and accept responsibility. Now in Chapters 19 and 20 we contemplate a commitment to action.

For the financially distressed organization, life in the Zone of Insolvency is increasingly fraught with risk due to the regulatory focus on board accountability. The board can be held legally responsible for decisions made in the Zone of Insolvency that advantage one party of the corporation while disadvantaging another. This is new territory since the 1992 court ruling, setting boards up to be second-guessed on all kinds of decisions. Balancing the interests of all parties of the corporation demands the wisdom of Solomon and then some. Historically, those who have served on nonprofit boards have needed to accept a level of financial distress that they would not tolerate in their for-profit businesses. This has been a dominant theme in the nonprofit culture, as organizations have stretched and sacrificed to maximize their service offerings, helping the most people for the lowest possible cost. Financial distress has been a badge of honor for many nonprofits. Some of these organizations will go so far as to state that they are philosophically opposed to building cash reserves or ending a fiscal year with any net gains.

If governance in the Zone of Insolvency is fraught with increasing risks, then it would seem logical to make a commitment not to live in the Zone of Insolvency. As a practical matter, however, this nation's social services support system would be in chaos if this resulted in every financially distressed nonprofit serving the sector filing for dissolution. The challenge for a decision not to live in the Zone of Insolvency is a challenge to raise the bar and move organizations away from financial distress into fiscal strength. As we saw in Chapters 15 and 16, there is much to be learned from the operating characteristics common to financially strong organizations as well as to financially weak organizations. Undoubtedly there are some financially distressed nonprofits that have lost their market effectiveness; they would best serve the nonprofit community at large by arranging a merger or filing for dissolution. For the great majority of nonprofits, the decision to raise the bar for fiscal strength and deliberately escape from or avoid the Zone of Insolvency is the decision that will best serve the public.

Clearly this raises questions about the causes and implications of financial distress. Does the financial distress of a nonprofit enhance its ability to serve? Is living on the edge an appropriate badge of honor for a nonprofit? Would the ability to serve be denigrated by a fiscally strong organization? Will donors give only to financially distressed nonprofits? Would donors refuse to give to the same organization if it generated modest reserves to strengthen its long-term viability and position it to serve the mission in the future? Is financial distress an inevitable reality for most nonprofits? Can a nonprofit escape from, or avoid, the Zone of Insolvency with a commitment to action?

WE WILL NOT LIVE IN THE ZONE OF INSOLVENCY

Regardless of the current financial status of your organization, it will benefit from a strong commitment by board and management that states "We will not live in the Zone of Insolvency." This commitment will create a focus for many discussions and decisions. Every decision should reinforce the commitment. It has a solid basis in the assessment (Chapter 17) and acknowledgment (Chapter 18). Future decisions should become proofs of this commitment.

EVERY DECISION WE MAKE WILL BE A PROOF OF THIS COMMITMENT

"We will not live in the Zone of Insolvency. Every decision we make will be a proof of this commitment." All decisions by board and management should be evaluated against the commitment not to live in the Zone of Insolvency. Whether considering a new lease, buying or selling real estate, upgrading office technology, building a new building, purchasing a new vehicle, hiring or terminating staff, developing the new strategic plan, or setting next year's budget, ask the question: "Will this decision move us away from or toward the Zone of Insolvency?"

WE WILL FIX IT, MERGE IT, OR FILE FOR DISSOLUTION

"We will not live in the Zone of Insolvency. Every decision we make will be a proof of this commitment. We will fix it, merge it, or file for dissolution." There are only three alternatives to living in financial distress: build fiscal strength, arrange for a merger, or file for dissolution. The public is best served by fiscally viable, ongoing nonprofits. In rare instances, the public may be best served by dissolution or merger of an organization that has lost its market effectiveness. The objective of this book is to rally board and management to strengthen the fiscal position of individual organizations and thereby strengthen the $3 trillion public trust represented by all nonprofits combined.

Establishing specific goals with timelines is key to the commitment process. Based on your assessment of the current state of the organization and your acknowledgment of the responsibility of board and management, commit to specific changes by specific dates. For instance, a commitment to develop next year's budget with a net gain instead of a net loss, along with a commitment to achieve the budget goal, may be a significant commitment for some organizations. For others that have typically delivered net gains, the commitment may be to increase the net, or to begin funding depreciation, or to build a research and development fund into next year's budget. The commitment must be specific; it must include timelines and establish a process for implementation and monitoring of actual reality versus goal sought for.

Finally, a serious commitment of the board will address accountability. How will the board hold itself and management accountable for honoring the commitment? What will be the consequences of failure? Is there a board committee or officer that will raise the flag for accountability?

Five Great Questions for Your Next Board Meeting

1. Have we as a board demonstrated adequate commitment to avoiding or escaping from the Zone of Insolvency?
2. In what ways must we demonstrate a new level of commitment to the fiscal condition of the organization?
3. If we are making a new commitment to build fiscal strength, how will we measure success?
4. What will be the consequences if this board fails to commit to building financial strength?
5. What will be our greatest challenge as we try to honor our commitment to avoid or escape from the Zone of Insolvency?

CHAPTER 20

Action

United States Marine Corps (retired) Major General Thomas L. Wilkerson was invited to meet with the board of the U.S. Naval Institute (USNI), a membership organization founded in 1873, embedded at the Naval Academy in Annapolis, Maryland. USNI was in financial distress. The board had dismissed the CEO and wanted General Wilkerson to take over as CEO and "fix it." With 31 years of service in the Marine Corps, including over 3,000 hours accident-free flight time in the F4 Phantom and the F/A-18 Hornet, and having served as commander of the largest command in the Corps, with over 100,000 Marines at 200 sites, General Wilkerson was no shrinking violet. After hearing out the board's proposal, the general suggested that to blame all of the financial woes of the Naval Institute on the previous CEO was to understate the board's fiduciary responsibilities. He then offered that he would accept the CEO position provided that every member of the board resign so that he could rebuild the organization with a board that understood its fiduciary role, including members from outside of the Navy.

General Wilkerson is a man of action, in battle, in the command center, and in the boardroom. The general refused to put himself in peril of a repeat performance by a board that did not recognize its own primary role as fiduciary, with the board again blaming the CEO for the financial woes of the organization. Better to report to a visionary board that understands and accepts its fiduciary role, a board that will delegate responsibilities, hold management accountable, and govern by policy.

Moving an organization out of the Zone of Insolvency demands an action plan. Without an assessment, acknowledgment, commitment, and action plan, the financially distressed nonprofit will continue perpetually in the Zone of Insolvency or fall through the zone to bankruptcy and dissolution. Living perpetually in the Zone of Insolvency, by design or by default, is increasingly risky given both current public sentiment and case law pushing for increasing levels of board accountability. The likelihood of being prosecuted in the line of volunteer service on a nonprofit board has never been greater.

Let's review the actions of the 10 organizations described in our opening case studies.

United Way of America: Reactive and Solvent

The board of the United Way of America reacted to media pressure regarding Richard Aramony's alleged behavior and stood by their man, rejecting his resignation. When Aramony was prosecuted and the board realized it had been betrayed, it became proactive in establishing systems to minimize potential for future abuse. The organization avoided the Zone of Insolvency, but incurred millions of dollars of expenses related to the scandal and lost hundreds of millions of dollars in charitable gifts.

Foundation for New Era Philanthropy: Not Active and Bankrupt

It is not clear that there was ever a functioning board for the foundation. The organization had no commitment to solvency, and it appears to have been totally inept in regard financial management. It lived its short life totally in the Zone of Insolvency and ended in bankruptcy.

Allegheny Health, Education and Research Foundation: Proactive and Bankrupt

AHERF was aggressively proactive in planning financial growth but dysfunctional in governance and accountability, falling quickly through the Zone of Insolvency to bankruptcy and criminal prosecution.

National Alliance of Business: Proactive and Dissolved

The National Alliance of Business was fiscally strong; it avoided the Zone of Insolvency and was proactive in its decision to close with net assets for distribution to member organizations.

United Way National Capital Region: Reactive and into the Zone of Insolvency

The United Way National Capital Region board was surprised by the illegal behavior of the long-term CEO and reacted to the situation to ensure it would not happen again. The organization had significant expenses related to the scandal; it lost tens of millions of dollars in charitable gifts income and continues to drift in and out of the Zone of Insolvency.

Baptist Foundation of Arizona: Proactive and Bankrupt

The board of the Baptist Foundation of Arizona was aggressively proactive in pursuit of financial growth, but failed at holding itself or its executives accountable. Inside trading and conflicts of interest were common, and juvenile and risky investment strategies landed it in the Zone of Insolvency and ultimately led to total insolvency and bankruptcy.

Western Fairfax Christian Ministries: Reactive and into the Zone of Insolvency

The board of the Western Fairfax Christian Ministries was proactive in regard to moving to larger facilities, but would have been served by more caution in regard to expanding the fixed overhead expenses. As a result, it ended up reacting to the financial crisis and drifted into the Zone of Insolvency.

AMERICAN RED CROSS: PROACTIVE AND SOLVENT

The Orange County Chapter of the American Red Cross was proactive in investigating and prosecuting an accountant who embezzled funds. Its proactive stance was respected by donors, and the organization continues in fiscal strength today, avoiding the Zone of Insolvency.

ELECTRONIC INDUSTRIES ASSOCIATION: PROACTIVE AND DISSOLVED

The board of the Electronic Industries Association was proactive in deciding that even though it had tens of millions of dollars in net assets, it had served its purpose and should be dissolved. Avoiding the Zone of Insolvency, in dissolution it will be able to distribute its multimillion-dollar assets to the five member nonprofit organizations better poised to carry the mission forward.

WOMEN IN COMMUNITY SERVICE: REACTIVE AND BANKRUPT

The board of Women in Community Service tried every means to keep the organization alive, but ultimately reacted to major reductions in contract income, falling through the Zone of Insolvency and filing for bankruptcy.

QUESTIONNAIRE LEADING TO AN ACTION PLAN

1. What is your organization's action plan to avoid or emerge from the Zone of Insolvency?
2. Do you need to reduce operating expenses to generate an annual net gain?
3. Should you hire business development staff to generate new fee-based income?
4. Is it time to start booking and funding depreciation?
5. Would you benefit from establishing a research and development fund?
6. Does the board need to get serious about policy governance and accountability?
7. Is your debt ratio too high and creating an unsustainable budget burden?

8. Could you invest your assets more aggressively for a higher social return?

9. Are you underpaying staff but overspending due to inadequate staff skills?

10. Is your product life cycle mix out of control and ready to drop you off a cliff?

11. Have you lost your position in the market because of environmental changes?

12. Does your organization continue in operation because it can or because it should?

13. If you are governing an organization in the Zone of Insolvency, are you effectively balancing all of the interests of all parties of the corporation?

14. If you were to close the organization today, do you have the assets to pay for all wind-down expenses?

15. If you were to close the organization today, what would be the net asset remaining after paying all wind-down expenses, and where could that be put to best use?

The questions will be different for every organization, and the action plans will differ by organization. Following are three sample action plans, one for a solvent organization, one for an organization in the Zone of Insolvency, and one for an insolvent organization. These are illustrative only; your organization needs its own customized action plan based on its unique situation. Keep it simple, and monitor progress regularly, and start today!

SAMPLE ACTION PLAN NO. I: FOR A SOLVENT NONPROFIT ORGANIZATION

Goal

We will double our client base in five years.

Strategy

We will begin to invest a portion of our net assets in research and development to develop and launch new products that will generate additional fee-for-service income and thereby support servicing an expanded client base.

Rationale

We are operating in a position of financial strength and believe it is prudent to continue to build net assets to a reasonable level, not to exceed 120% of annual operating expenses. Beyond that level, we believe it is prudent to invest in research and development to launch new self-sustaining products and services that will expand the level of service to current clients and expand the client base.

Metrics for Success

- Maintain net assets in a range equal to 100% to 120% of annual operating expenses.
- Annually invest equivalent of 3% to 6% of operating expenses on research and development.
- Build and maintain research and development fund in the range equivalent to 20% to 25% of annual operating expenses within three years.
- Generate returns in excess of investment within three years.

Tactics with Timelines

- Inform the board and obtain necessary approvals at the next board meeting.
- Establish initial research and development fund by allocating funds equal to 10% of annual operating expense at the beginning of the next budget cycle.
- Establish and post criteria and protocols whereby staff and other interested parties can apply for research and development funds to develop and launch new products or services—to be completed and posted by June 1.
- Establish research and development review committee prior to new budget cycle to assess all requests for funds against established criteria; committee will be empowered to award funds up to specific predetermined levels.

Accountability

Chair of research and development review committee will file quarterly reports listing funding requests, status, funds approved, and returns on investment each quarter to management and board.

Strategy approved for initial period of three years with expectation that returns will exceed investment by end of the third year. Board reserves the right to change the strategy if progress toward the goal is not evident or if returns do not exceed investment after three years.

SAMPLE ACTION PLAN NO. 2: FOR A NONPROFIT ORGANIZATION IN THE ZONE OF INSOLVENCY

Goal

We will work ourselves out of the Zone of Insolvency within one year.

Strategy

We will break even this year and generate annual net gains in the range of 7% to 10% of annual operating expenses beginning next year.

Rationale

We believe that the organization is viable, is serving its mission, and should continue in operation. We have been living with perpetual financial distress and believe that it is prudent and necessary to move out of this zone for the long-term good of the organization.

Metrics for Success

- Manage budget to annual net gains of 7% to 10%.
- Meet seasonal cash flow needs without commercial borrowing.
- Increase net assets by at least 20% per year until net assets are equal to a range of 100% to 120% of annual expenses.
- Transition to totally funded depreciation within three years.

Tactics with Timelines

- Sell 80 acres of undeveloped land and put cash toward funding depreciation and building operating cash reserve (sale pending with closing anticipated by December).

- Implement new compensation plan in next budget cycle to upgrade staff skills, increasing total compensation by reducing base pay, and adding a performance plan that ensures net gains for the organization in return for incentive pay.
- Conduct comprehensive review of all vendor contracts and negotiate better terms based on competitive bid protocols, for completion by July.
- Immediately discontinue three products that have generated net losses during the past five years.

Accountability

Board will hold the CEO accountable for this goal and for individual metrics as outlined. The CEO will assure that every employee has written performance expectations, and performance compensation incentives will focus on desired outcome.

SAMPLE ACTION PLAN NO. 3: FOR AN INSOLVENT NONPROFIT ORGANIZATION

Goal

We will file arrange for a merger with another nonprofit of similar mission by year's end.

Strategy

We understand that it is unlikely that any other organization will want to take us on in a merger if all they acquire is debt. However, we are in discussions with a sister organization that is interested in acquiring our client network to add volume to theirs and thereby make their organization more business viable by increasing volume and proportionately reducing fixed overhead expenses. It appears that if we time the merger to coincide with our annual fundraising event in March, we could be debt free at the time of the merger. Furthermore, we believe that by announcing the merger at our annual fundraising event, we will actually increase funds raised at the event, as this announcement will be very positively received by our constituents.

Rationale

We believe that our organization is serving a legitimate need in the community, but our inability to grow to a size that would justify our overhead suggests that we would serve more effectively as a program of a larger organization.

Metrics for Success

One year after the merger, more people will be served by the merged organization than were previously served by the two organizations acting separately.

The merged organization will operate with a net annual gain of 7% to 10% beginning year one.

All debt will be eliminated prior to the merger so that the new organization starts out debt free.

1. Negotiate a written agreement of intent to merge, approved by both boards no later than October.
2. Manage wind-down expenses and the annual fundraising event so that the organization is debt free at the time of the merger.
3. Complete the merger and announce it publicly at the March event.

Accountability

The board will discipline itself and hold management accountable to achieve the debt-free merger as scheduled. Moving forward, the new merged organization will include three of our board members on the new board to assure continuity of mission.

It is appropriate that this book ends with a call to action based on a review of case studies, an understanding of the issues, organizational assessment, acknowledgment, and commitment. As the case studies have demonstrated, all boards are well served by a healthy dose of skepticism and a commitment to accountability. Without action, nothing will change. Building board consensus to take action is not necessarily easy, especially on the large issues. But the board that fails to act to avoid or escape the Zone of Insolvency does so at its own risk.

This is not a message of gloom and doom. It is not a call to dismiss or dissolve large numbers of nonprofit organizations. Rather, the call to action is an attempt to raise the bar and strengthen the complete community of nonprofits for the good of the public at large. The nonprofit sector is a national treasure, and we can each play a role in strengthening the good work of the nonprofit community.

May the path you choose make your organization financially viable well into the future and lead to comfort, support, and blessings for those you serve.

FIVE GREAT QUESTIONS FOR YOUR NEXT BOARD MEETING

1. What action will we take to avoid or escape the Zone of Insolvency?
2. What will be the greatest obstacle to success?
3. How will our action plan be helped or hindered by this organization's corporate culture?
4. What new resources are essential to the successful implementation of our action plans?
5. How will we celebrate success?

CHAPTER 21

Conclusion

The courts have recently defined expanded legal responsibilities for those managing and governing organizations in the Zone of Insolvency.

Approximately 450,000 nonprofit organizations are unaware that they are operating in the Zone of Insolvency.

Millions of nonprofit board members and managers are unaware of their corporate and individual legal liabilities as they govern organizations in the Zone of Insolvency.

Board members can be held personally liable for their actions while governing in the Zone of Insolvency, including decisions that result in failure to pay taxes or wages, selling property for less than fair value, or violations of ERISA.

Given the current-day focus on corporate accountability (Sarbanes-Oxley, Nonprofit Integrity Act of California, the Zone of Insolvency), nonprofit board members and executives must exercise extraordinary diligence to comply with the law and minimize their liabilities.

The nonprofit culture that has tolerated or even embraced perpetual financial distress must now deal with the current-day risks of governing in the Zone of Insolvency.

There are three ways out of the Zone of Insolvency: building financial strength, arranging a merger, or filing for dissolution.

Every nonprofit organization, regardless of its current financial status, must have an action plan to avoid or escape from the Zone of Insolvency.

Index